# The transformation of the Prokuratura into a body compatible with the democratic principles of law

proceedings

Multilateral meeting
organised by the Council of Europe with
the co-operation of the Office of the Prosecutor General
of the Republic of Hungary

Budapest, 27-29 September 1994

Programme: Themis 2

Council of Europe legal co-operation with
central and eastern European countries

Council of Europe Publishing, 1996

French edition:

*La transformation de la Prokuratura en instance compatible avec les principes démocratiques de justice*

ISBN 92-871-2943-6

Council of Europe Publishing
F-67075 Strasbourg Cedex

ISBN 92-871-2944-4
© Council of Europe, 1996
Printed in Germany

## INDEX

**Opening speeches**

Mr. Árpád GÖNCZ, President of the Republic of Hungary . . . . . . . . . . . . . . . . . 5

Mr Pál VASTAGH, Minister of Justice of the Republic of Hungary . . . . . . . . . . 7

Mrs. Marie-Odile WIEDERKEHR, Deputy Director of Legal Affairs,
Council of Europe . . . . . . . . . . . . . . . . . . . . . . . . . . . . . . . . . . . . . . . . . . . . . . 9

*Introductory lecture: the Public Prosecutor's Office in the transnational period*

Dr. Kálmán GYÖRGY, Prosecutor General of Hungary . . . . . . . . . . . . . . . . . . 13

**Topic 1:** *The constitutional status and the internal structure of the Public Prosecution in a State governed by the rule of law*

José Manuel SANTOS PAIS, Public Prosecutor (Portugal) . . . . . . . . . . . . . . . . 25

Mr. Attila HLAVATY, Director of the Secretariat of the Public Prosecutor
General's Office of Hungary . . . . . . . . . . . . . . . . . . . . . . . . . . . . . . . . . . . . . . 39

**Topic 2:** *Selection and status of prosecutors and the management of the prosecutor's office*

Mr. François CORDIER, Premier substitut du Procureur de la République
de Paris (France) . . . . . . . . . . . . . . . . . . . . . . . . . . . . . . . . . . . . . . . . . . . . . . . 49

Mrs Iiona LÉVAI, Head of Division, Prosecutor General's Office of Hungary . . 79

**Topic 3:** *Prosecutorial functions in connection with criminal law: pre-trial functions; discretionary power; trial functions*

Mrs Birgitte VESTBERG, Staatsadvokaten for Fyn (Denmark) . . . . . . . . . . . . . 87

Mr. Endre BÓCZ, Prosecutor General of Budapest (Hungary) . . . . . . . . . . . . . 95

**TOPIC 4:** *The role of prosecutors in the application of international criminal law; mutual assistance in criminal matters, transfer of criminal proceedings, extradition, etc.*

Peter WILKITZKI, Ministerialrat, Ministry of Justice (Germany) .......... 101

Mr. Lásló LÁNG, Director, Prosecutor General's Office (Hungary) ......... 109

**TOPIC 5:** *Functions of the public prosecutor's office in connection with civil litigations and its extra judicial functions*

Mr. Christian PAUL-LOUBIERE, Magistrat at the Tribunal de Grande Instance of Paris (France) .............................................. 115

Mrs Nóra Katalin BONOMI, Prosecutor, Prosecutor General's Office (Hungary) 137

Mr. Jerzy SZYMANSKI, Prosecutor, Prosecutor General's Office of Appeal (Poland) .............................................................. 145

***Conclusions and Recommendations*** ............................. 151

Programme ................................................................. 157

List of Participants ........................................................ 163

> **Address of welcome by**
>
> **Mr. Árpád GONCZ**
> **President of the Republic of Hungary**

Ladies and Gentlemen!

It is a great pleasure for me to welcome you to the joint scientific event of the Council of Europe and the Chief Prosecution of the Republic of Hungary, because for me, this form of organisation represents an eloquent testimony and a practical incarnation of our European cooperation endeavours.

As a direct result of the political actions having taken place in the region, the administrative and political leadership of European countries has been concerned about the problems of the prosecutions of Central and Eastern Europe countries for a long time now, which is due to both its legal-theoretical and obvious political consequences.

The constitutional status of the prosecution as well as its role in the public administration relate to the basic guarantees of civil democracies. As such, its constitutional position and authority is one of the measures of a civil society's development. This makes it clear that any debates with regard to the issue cannot be degraded to the level of everyday politics.

The actual legislative solutions that are provided for in fundamental laws have to be based on perfect models with democratic values, as well as on professional forums like this.

The intention of the Council of Europe, namely to provide for an international forum to discuss the related essential issues and to exchange views on a Europe-wide basis, is an invaluable service to both the region and Hungary, for which I would hereby also like to express my thanks.

The meeting organised by the Council of Europe and the Federal Ministry of Justice of Austria in May 1993 in Vienna, which can be regarded as antecedents to the present conference, arrived at the conclusion that the concrete exchange of views by the countries concerned in the political transformation, consultation with these countries, and detailed analyses of their situation are all indispensable to establish optimal administrative solutions. At the same time, consultation can lead to lessons, which may serve the modernisation of existing models in Europe.

Having reviewed the programme of this conference, I am confident that it will embrace the entire spectrum of the constitutional state, organisation and authority of the prosecution as well as the legal status of prosecutors, hence we will all have a comprehensive view on problems and possible solutions as a result of this conference.

As far as I know, European prosecutors have never met in such a large number since the establishment of the prosecution's institution. This, in addition to negotiating important professional issues, provides an excellent opportunity to establish and tighten personal relations.

I wish you that you take advantage of this opportunity, and you have a nice time in Hungary and in the company of your fellow professionals. I wish you every success to your valuable work.

## Address of welcome by

## Mr Pál VASTAGH
### Minister of Justice of the Republic of Hungary

Ladies and Gentlemen!
Dear participants of the International Conference!

I am pleased to comply with your honourable invitation. I consider it extremely important myself that views are regularly exchanged on the organisation of the prosecution and its present and future scope of duties and authority with the broad participation of both scientific people and the users of the law. I also find it essential that professional scientific debates including international conferences should increase in number on this question. As you all know it very well, the topicality of the issue is justified by the fact that the coalition agreement of the winning parties on the summer parliamentary elections, as well as the resulting government programme are involved in the necessity to elaborate the new Constitution as one of their priorities. I would not like to dwell on the direction of the process of Constitution now, since this is far beyond the scope of the issue to be discussed. I have to underline, however, that in the course of the preparation of the new Constitution, those political and professional debates, which have related to the constitutional status of the prosecution during the past few years, practically since the first day of the 1989-90 transformation process, should be concluded.

As you all know it very well, the Government made a resolution in August on the preparation of the process of Constitution. In this resolution, it commissioned the Ministry of Justice to conclude a scientific research agreement with the Institute of State and Legal Sciences of the Hungarian Academy of Sciences, in order to elaborate studies in support of the new Constitution, and to prepare a scientific constitutional concept based on the part-studies carried out. Some of the most significant representatives of scientific public life have been awarded contracts of assignment to expound on specific fields of the Constitution in their studies. It has been indicated that scientific papers are being prepared also on the theoretical models of the prosecution. I do believe that at the end of the process of Constitution, models acceptable to all and based on full consensus will be composed in regard to the constitutional structure of each of the crucial constitutional organisations, such as the prosecution.

Though those being present know it, I shortly still have to mention the two models which have been at issue during the past few years as regards to the constitutional state of the prosecution. Practically, one of the models is the prosecution with today's constitutional status, that is, such a centralised organisation which is exclusively related to the Parliament via the chief prosecutor. As you all know, the chief prosecutor can be interpellated and called upon before the Parliament in the current legal structure. The competing constitutional models connects the prosecution to the executive power through the chief prosecutor and the minister of Justice, and basically places it under the supervision of the Government. In regard to both models, the authority of the prosecution is an issue to be dealt with separately. Some would reduce it to its classic authority, which is essentially not more than representing the prosecution. Others propose to keep the majority of its authority today, one of the basic elements of which is similar to the Austrian public health activity. Obviously, as far as its authority is concerned, it is impossible to decide in favour of either models on the basis of simple vote, or purely tastes and likes. It is scientific investigations that can substantiate a final decision and put the constituting power in a decision-making situation. Nevertheless, when examining European models and European legal practices, it can be stated that even in those countries, where the prosecution has operated under governmental supervision until recently, there is a strong intention to render it independent of the government. Indeed, a constitutionally guaranteed separation from the executive power has already taken place in a number of instances.

I am confident that during the development of the concept of the Constitution and some specific issues, the jurisprudential people can count on the intellectual capacity having accumulated at prosecutors' offices and prosecutors. I hereby offer, too, that in addition to taking part in the work process, the constitutional concept be forwarded to the chief prosecutor for his general and special statement. We would consider it an honour if along with the official and hierarchical reporting of the prosecutors' profession, a reconciliation from a different point of view were held. More precisely, I am thinking of the National Association of Prosecutors as an interest representative body. I a certain that the prosecutors could also support the contents of the chief prosecutor's opinion in such a different role of theirs. It is also possible, however, that as a representative body, they consider different angles and form different statements.

Finally, I would like to express how pleased I was to learn that the early establishment of the International Association of Prosecutors will be an important milestone and a remarkable event in the new dimensions of international communication. Considerable responsibility falls on the Council of Europe to assist the formation. Having heard of the initiatives, from the point of view of the country and the Hungarian prosecutors, it would be a great honour for Budapest to seat the new organisation. As far as I am concerned, I would hereby like to publicly offer the possibility of a harmonious cooperation to both the management of the Chief Prosecution and the organisation of the prosecutors' self-government — which otherwise the chief prosecutor and me agreed on in words following my appointment as minister of justice.

Dear participants of the International Conference, I wish that your work together, the professional consultation will be successful and hope that at the end of the sometimes exhausting process of Constitution, such a consensus-based structure of prosecution will be established, which is able to fulfil its various and far-reaching duties as a state authority at high standards, and provides a pleasant atmosphere for the employees of the strengthening Prosecutors' self-government.

> **Opening speech by**
>
> **Mrs. Marie-Odile WIEDERKEHR**
> **Deputy Director of Legal Affairs**
> **at the Council of Europe**

The President of the Republic,
the Minister of Justice,
the Principal State Prosecutor,
Ladies and Gentleman,

1. I would like to take this opportunity to express the Council of Europe's gratitude to the Hungarian authorities who have been so kind as to assist it in organising this important conference bringing together representatives of 16 Central and Eastern European states. Our Secretary General, Mr Daniel Tarchys, has asked me to thank you, Mr President, for your hospitality and in particular for your presence and regrets that he himself cannot be in Budapest today. I am sure that thanks to the exemplary co-operation established between the Council of Europe and the Hungarian authorities, in particular the Principal State Prosecutor's Department, this conference will be an event of considerable importance not only for states who have applied to become members of the Council of Europe but also to those who are already members, for there is always progress to be made in the field of democracy and human rights.

2. The subject which brings us together here in Budapest - a city we are always delighted to visit - is not only of prime importance in a democratic society but, like all matters concerning democracy, requires a broad-minded approach encouraging a tactful exchange of opinions, whereby we should take into account both the principles and standards of the rule of law and the character and traditions of each of our countries. There is no single model in this field which can be incorporated as such into the legal system of all member states of the Council of Europe and consequently recommended to would-be member states.

3. At the same time it is important not to underestimate the importance of the Prosecution Service in a democracy founded on the rule of law.

In democracies which are by their very nature fragile, particularly when they are newly-established, the task of the Prosecution Service - consisting mainly of instituting and conducting criminal proceedings in cases where the law has been violated -directly concerns the defence of the whole system of democratic institutions. As Mr

Siegfried MÜLLENBACH, Advocate-General to the German Federal Court of Justice, so rightly said in Bucharest in May this year, the Prosecution Service represents the interests of the state, which are at one and the same time the interests of the Government and of the citizens who are members of a society living under the rule of law. On account of this dual role, the Prosecution Service can take the side of neither the state nor the accused and must endeavour to be as objective as possible. He added that on the one hand public prosecutors must endeavour to establish the truth and impose the corresponding penalties on those guilty while, on the other hand, they must also disclose any evidence which might discharge the accused. They must ensure that legal rules are strictly applied during the criminal proceedings, that those who are guilty suffer the consequences and that those who are innocent are not prosecuted.

4. The public prosecutor therefore plays an essential role in the prevention of crime which has since the very beginning been one of the main aims of the Council of Europe. The large number of conventions in the field of criminal law, which in turn reflect the provisions of the European Convention of Human Rights and the decisions handed down by its organs, bear witness to this. Work in this field will inevitable increase, for it is obvious that the adoption of criminal laws showing due regard for human rights and adapted to the evolution of modern societies and the introduction of judicial institutions which can apply these laws are of prime importance especially in nascent democracies,.

5. In order to perform its task, the prosecution service must establish its role in a democratic society founded on the separation of powers.

Another expert on the realities of law, Mr Eugène FRENCKEN, the Secretary General of the Belgian Ministry of Justice, recently put the questions which must be addressed if one is seeking to establish the exact role of the prosecution service in a democratic society in the following words:

"Is it necessary to create a totally independent or relatively autonomous prosecution service if its role is not to hand down judgments, this being the exclusive role of judges?
Should it be subject to the authority of the Ministry of Justice if it participates in the application of the law which by nature entails total independence from the political powers? Such difficulties are never-ending and require constant attention as our societies develop".

6. Apart from the divergencies - to put it mildly - in the organisation of prosecution services in the different European countries, the principle of the separation of powers serves as a basic guideline which clearly entails the exclusion of any kind of general supervision of the legality of decisions taken by bodies answerable to other authorities as there was in the past. The possibility of the prosecution service performing other duties than those concerning criminal proceedings needs to be examined not only in the light of this requirement but also of the traditions I referred to before.

7. The eminent public prosecutors and the members of their departments as well as the representatives of ministries of justice gathered here today are therefore invited to continue their examination of these problems. The Budapest Conference indeed follows on from another conference held in Vienna just over a year ago at the invitation of the Austrian authorities and from a series of bilateral seminars organised by the Council of Europe in the various countries concerned.

We should now be able to take our work a step further thanks to the excellent questionnaire that was distributed in advance and which has almost all the aspects of the role of public prosecutors in a democracy. The work done by a majority of the representatives of the countries of Central and Eastern Europe in answering this questionnaire deserves our praise. The resulting picture is a complex one on account of both the diversity of solutions adopted in the different countries and of the different levels of awareness of the problems. Some replies openly acknowledge that only part of the work has been achieved, other countries which are further along the road to reform have described the various stages enabling them to establish institutions which are compatible with the democratic principles of law, in accordance with the title of this conference.

8. To resume the words of an Austrian philosopher, Karl POPPER, who died recently, our trials and errors may constitute a valuable experience if we are modest enough to acknowledge them and discuss them with others. This should be the spirit of the dialogue of the next three days. I, for my part, am convinced that, thanks to the experience and exceptional knowledge of all the participants here today, the Budapest Conference will provide a better understanding of a key institution in our societies and enable us to adopt conclusions and recommendations which will enhance the progress of democracy and the rule of law in Europe.

# INTRODUCTORY LECTURE

# THE PUBLIC PROSECUTOR'S OFFICE IN THE TRANSITIONAL PERIOD

### Dr. Kálmán GYÖRGY
### Prosecutor General of Hungary

Mr Chairman,
Honourable Guests from the Council of Europe,
Distinguished Colleagues,
Ladies and Gentlemen,

By way of introduction let me remind you of the fact that the constitutional position of the Hungarian Public Prosecutor's Office did not change during the historic period çot the late 80's and early 90's. For the time being, the prosecutorial organisation in Hungary is an independent body subordinated only to the law and connected only to the Parliament through the person of the Prosecutor General. This solution was inherited from the old regime and until now has not been expressly confirmed neither rejected by the freely elected legislatures.

In other words, a final political decision in this respect has not been taken yet by the Parliament. Moreover, there are controversies about the scope of functions the Public Prosecutor's Office should exercise. In sum, there are a lot of questions to be answered and a lot of problems to be settled. Consequently, it would hardly be an exaggeration to say that this is the most propitious time for us to analyse and discuss the theoretical and practical problems of the Public Prosecutor's Office.

A number of key issues arise from the constitutional position itself which cannot be separated from the requirements of the democratic principles of law. Of course, several approaches are possible and different aspects of these issues can be examined.

Please allow me to put these issues in a little bit broader context, and confine myself mainly to one aspect which can be summarized as follows: how is it possible to ensure for the Public Prosecutor's Office the necessary impartiality and the objectivity when exercising its functions? According to many recommendations and resolutions adopted by different international organizations and scholarly meetings, the impartiality and the objectivity are the two main requirements prosecutors should meet. It is obvious that the key issues have very important human right implications as well. In this respect, the principles of impartiality and objectivity mean an additional human right dimension to the main issues which are mostly of constitutional character.

After these preliminary remarks, the broad outlines of the subject I would like to deal with are as follows:

- the main characteristics of the so-called "Prokuratura";

- the specific development and problems of the Hungarian Public Prosecutor's Office in the transitional period;

- some peculiarities and principles related to the Public Prosecutor's Office;

- the inspiration we can take from other public prosecution systems in order to guarantee the impartiality and objectivity and to meet other requirements of a democratic society.

## I.

I think, the organ named "Prokuratura" in the title of our meeting means the so-called "Public Prosecutor's Office of the socialist type" established on the Soviet model in all Soviet bloc countries after World War II. By no means I would like to insult my colleagues, including my Austrian or Scottish friends, whose prosecutorial organs, for historical reasons and in accordance with their legal traditions, bear such names as Prokuratura or Procurator Fiscal Service.

We all know that the origin of the Russian Prokuratura dates back to the era of Peter the Great who in 1722 took over the French model in order to have an efficient control organ, "an eye of the monarch" supervising central and local administrative authorities. The Prokuratura of this type was replaced in 1864 by a new institution which also followed the French model of the time and have prosecutorial tasks only. This institution was considered as one of the symbols of tsarism and was abolished in 1918.

The Soviet Prokuratura, established in 1922 meant a return to the old traditions prior to 1864: the function of supervising law observance beyond the sphere of criminal law was resumed. The general supervision of legality covered the acts of the executive, local Soviets, economic enterprises, mass organizations, public officials, courts, etc. The aim of this function was to ensure a strict and uniform law enforcement and law observance all over the empire.

When comparing the Prokuratura of the Soviet type with other models, Western authors usually find two typical features which distinguish the "Prokuratura" from the Western model. One is its constitutional position: since 1936 the Prokuratura of the Soviet type was a totally autonomous organ, depending directly and exclusively from the highest legislative organ. The other is the enormous general supervisory power exercised over almost all areas of state functioning and social life, especially in the former Soviet Union.

However, it is worth stating at this point that the organizational autonomy and independence of the Public Prosecutor Office from the executive also exists in certain Western countries. Furthermore, it should not be left out of consideration that in Finland, for example, the independent Chancellor of Justice, who is the highest prosecuting authority, also has a wide power of general supervisory control over legality. It would be difficult to state that these countries have a Public Prosecutor's Office of Soviet type incompatible with the democratic principles of law.

What was the main problem with the "Prokuratura"? How can the specific characteristics of the Soviet model be identified?

I think, we should begin with the well-known fact that there is no dictatorial state which would be ready to admit the principle of the separation of powers. Such principles of Montesquieu as "there is no liberty, if the power of judging be not separated from the legislative and executive powers" could not be acceptable for any state of authorisation character. The communist doctrine propagated the principle of the unity of powers. In reality, all powers belonged to the one omnipotent party.

Despite these circumstances, each country of the Eastern bloc had a legislative body, a government, central and local administration, courts and Public Prosecutor Office. The problem reside in the fact that the existence of these organs represented only a certain distribution of functions within the state machine, and not a real separation of powers, where the mechanism of interdependence, checks and balances predominates. In fact, the political power was uncontrolled, the accountability of the different organs to each other and to the people was only a formality.

Consequently, under the conditions of the party-state the direct and exclusive subordination of the "Prokuratura" to the Parliament or another highest legislative body was of no real importance. Had it been subordinated to the executive or the judiciary, the result would not have changed: the political will of the communist party would have prevailed in any case. The office was part of a structure serving as an arrangement of stage, a certain facade for the legitimization of party rule.

On the other hand, the extension of the functions of the Public Prosecutor's Office reflected, to some extend, real needs. In Hungary, for instance, the general supervision of legality made up for a real shortcoming, since the so-called "socialist model of state organization" could not house such institutions as administrative courts, a Constitutional Court, Court of Audit or Ombudsman. Under these circumstances, general supervisory power of the prosecutor might be regarded, to some extent, as an instrument for the protection of individual rights. (It must be added that in Hungary the general supervisory power never covered the courts.)

Thus, we may even draw a conclusion that the root of the problem of the "Prokuratura" resides rather in the lack of a democratic environment, than in its constitutional position or in its scope of functions. The "Prokuratura" exercised its powers in a society which was deprived of such basic values as the pluralistic political democracy, the rule of law, free elections and the observance of human rights.

## II.

After the collapse of the old regimes, the political and social environment of the Public Prosecutor Office has suddenly and radically changed. As the first step in the transformation process, similarly to other countries of the region, constitutional measures were taken to depoliticize the office and to prevent any party affiliation on the part of the prosecutors. Several powers connected to the general supervision of legality have gradually been taken over by other organs or abrogated. Certain powers connected to civil cases have also been curtailed.

The terms of the Hungarian Constitution have become a reality: for at least four years the Public Prosecutor Office has been an entirely independent body, which is subject only to the law. In this context independence means that the office is independent from the Executive and the Judiciary and it is connected to the Parliament through the person of the Prosecutor General. The Prosecutor General is elected by and is accountable to Parliament.

It is obvious from this description that the constitutional position of the Public Prosecutor Office in Hungary has remained unchanged: it roughly follows the pattern of the "Prokuratura". Nevertheless, the responsibility of the Prosecutor General to the Parliament can no more be regarded as a mere formality, as it was the case during the years of the old regime.

The Members of Parliament may address the Prosecutor General with interpellation and ask him questions, and they do it quite frequently. The plenary session will vote on the Prosecutor General's answer. As a result, its position is somehow similar to that of a Minister, but with some differences which are not negligible. The Ministers are politically responsible to the Parliament and they may be interpellated on point of government policy, while the Prosecutor General is not a member of the Government, but he head of a depoliticized prosecutorial organization which is subjected only to the law. Surprisingly enough, the Prosecutor General very seldom is questioned on point of law, and very often on points that are political on the merit.

What is more, the Hungarian prosecuting system follows the principle of legality. Prosecutors, including the Prosecutor General, have no discretionary power to decide whether to prosecute or not. That is, the law prohibits the decision-making process to be politically influenced in any way. As the Prosecutor General is the guardian of law, his quasi-political responsibility to the Parliament in connection with pending criminal cases is a constitutional absurdity. (As one of my eminent colleagues point out recently, you can draw only two conclusions when an answer of the Prosecutor General, containing pure legal argumentation, is rejected by the Parliament: 1) the Prosecutor General does not properly know the law; 2) the Parliament does not agree with the law passed by itself.)

On the other hand, the Prosecutor General has the obligation to submit a report to the Parliament on his activities. Such reports shall be regularly submitted in many countries where the prosecutorial organization enjoys functional or total independence (for example England and Wales, Finland) and such reports provide the main constitutional means for legislature to control the overall prosecutorial activities. In Hungary, a general report covering several years' activities was already submitted to Parliament a few years ago, but the plenary session did not show very much interest. It was discussed only in standing committees.

All this brings us to a key issue which can be summarized as follows: which branch of power within the constitutional structure shall be responsible for such an important function of the State as the prosecution of crime and who shall bear the political responsibility for it before the Parliament?

The fact of the matter is that this issue seemed to be settled in 1990-91. According to a draft law elaborated at the time, the Public Prosecutor's Office would have been part of the executive branch, without loosing its internal autonomy, and the Minister of Justice would have been politically responsible for its functioning before the Parliament. The theoretical fundament of this solution consisted in the well-known German concept which states that in a democratic state acting under the rule of law the government must be accountable to the Parliament, but the government can only accept and fulfil the requirements resulting from this accountability if the subordinate authorities are subject to its control.

Consequently, this solution involved the external control of the Minister of Justice. His control would have comprised the right to give normative (general) instructions to direct prosecutorial activities on the one hand, and the right to give "positive" instructions to the Prosecutor General in individual cases, on the other hand. The Minister of Justice would not have been authorized to give "negative" instructions, i.e. instructions to refrain from acting, to dismiss the case, to drop the charge or to withdraw appeals.

It became clear soon that the draft law on the amendment of the constitutional position of the Public Prosecutor's Office would not be voted by the required two-third majority of Members of Parliament, since the parties represented in Parliament did not manage to reach a political consensus on the issue. Finally, all attempts to modify the constitutional position of the office have definitely aborted.

Surely the lesson to be learned from what has happened in this field during the last few years is that the issues connected to the constitutional position of the office are first and foremost political ones.

## III.

It is a commonplace that the modern Public Prosecutor's Office is a Napoleonic institution that served as a model for many countries in the Continental Europe during the XIXth century. In this model the prosecutorial organization is subordinated to the government, namely to the Minister of Justice. Yet, it is hard to read a work of a XIXth or a XXth century French author without being faced, directly or indirectly, with the question: what is the essence of the Public Prosecutor Office?

The main questions can be summarised as follows: is the office part of the executive or the judiciary? is the office an administrative organ or a judicial one? what kinds of interests are represented by the office: the interest of the government, the public interest or the interest of the law? The answers to these questions are primordial because they determine the place of the office in the constitutional structure, the scope of functions of the office and the status of the prosecutors.

What is quite certain is that is not easy to answer these questions. The Public Prosecutor's Office, even without being subordinated to the government, has a double character: prosecutors play an important role in the administration of justice which connects them to the courts, but prosecutors are also law enforcement officers, guardians of legality while performing extra-judicial and other functions. It is difficult to conceive the Public Prosecutor Office as a court composed of independent judges, and it is simply impossible to conceive it as a Ministry composed of public officials. It may be conceded that the office must be much closer to a court than to a Ministry.

One of the options to resolve this dilemma is to distinguish between the independence of the Office and that of the individual prosecutors. In most countries where the Office is subordinated to the executive, the status of prosecutors differs in many ways from the status of public officials. They usually enjoy more independence and more guarantees against the abuse of power of their internal or external superiors than public officials do. In short, their status is similar in many respects to the status of judges. In France, the prosecutors are "magistrats". In Germany, in cases prescribed by law they may refuse or must refuse to follow the instruction given by the superior, etc. Prosecutors must follow and be guided by judicial, and not political considerations.

I do not think the independence of the prosecutorial organization or the relative independence of prosecutors when performing their functions would result in a "fourth branch of power". It cannot be denied that the world has become more complex since Montesquieu and in the constitutional practice his theory on the strict separation of powers has been replaced by the interdependence of powers, especially in Europe. Even being so, it is worth mentioning what Montesquieu says about the prosecution: "a state authority [which] stands on guard instead of the citizens and acts. And the citizens remain calm." This authority, as Montesquieu explains, consists of officials ordered by the Prince to each court to prosecute all offenses in his name. We must not forget at that time the "Prince" incarnated both the legislative and the executive powers.

Nothing could be more true than what Mr. Strasser, President of the Austrian Prosecutor's Federation says: the prosecutorial organization is a *sui generis* institution, the only one of its own kind. This Janus-faced and peculiar institution is, as the German doctrine expresses it, a *justizverwaltungs organ* (a judicial-administrative body). Otherwise, members of the prosecutorial organization are obliged to act impartially, objectively and without any political influence.

It is an universal principle included in the United Nations Guidelines on the Role of Prosecutors adopted in 1990 that prosecutors shall perform their duties fairly and consistently, and uphold human rights, thus contributing to ensuring due process. In the performance of their duties, prosecutors shall carry out their functions impartially, and avoid all political, social, religious, racial, cultural or any other kind of discrimination. They shall protect the public interest and act with objectivity.

The XIVthe International Congress on Penal Law in 1989 also passed very important resolutions. It was emphasized that in a spirit of impartiality and objectiveness, the prosecution service must comply fully with its double role as guarantor of the application of law and as promoter of criminal process. In having such a possibility, the prosecution service can receive general directives of criminal policy. However, regarding specific cases it must exercise the administration of criminal justice in full independence. Furthermore, the judiciary must protect the individual against illegal or unjustified indictment.

It is interesting to consider how this impartiality and objectivity requirements can be ensured in certain systems.

## IV.

It is evident that most of us look to the solutions of Western democracies for inspiration in our reform efforts. The Pan-European Meeting on the transformation of the "Prokuratura" into a body compatible with the democratic principles of law, held in Vienna last year pointed out that there are many different prosecuting systems in Western Europe, but this should not produce confusion but choice. The picture is even more colourful, if we add some American solutions. This variety makes comparison somehow complicated, but not impossible.

Even though the constitutional position of the office is very important from this aspect, an approach limited to this issue would lead us to a generalization. We must choose a broader approach, because in reality the subject is extremely complex. Thus, the internal structure of the office, the prosecutorial discretion, provisions of the criminal procedure have also to be taken into consideration.

Let us begin with the French system. It is well known that French prosecutors serve in a centralized structure characterized by strictly hierarchical subordination, unity and indivisibility and headed by the Minister of Justice. The Minister of Justice has the power to give general guidelines as well as orders in individual cases to the prosecutors. All this is undeniably true, but the details need closer examination.

First, the structure of the criminal procedure differs considerably from that followed by most former Eastern bloc countries. In the latter the police and prosecutors have some quasi judicial powers which are equivalent to those of the French investigative judge. Second, the French prosecutor only at a very early stage of the criminal process is the real master of the case: when he decides whether to prosecute or not (classement sans suite). In sum, in the French procedure judicial power and control is much stronger than, for example, in the Hungarian one.

Third, the French prosecutor has a certain "own power" (pouvoir propre) which means that his decision may not be reversed even if it is directly contrary to the order of his superior. Since 1993 individual orders of the Minister of Justice should be given in written form and filed to the *dossier*. Furthermore, at the French trial "the pen is bound, but speech is free" which means that the prosecutor should follow the orders only in its written submissions, while in his oral observations he is absolutely free.

Fourth, the right of the victim (partie civile) to initiate procedure serves as a very important check on the actual or perceived abuses of the discretional power of the prosecutor to decline prosecution.

What is the rationale for the subordination of the Public Prosecutor Office to the Minister of Justice? The generally acknowledged reason for it is that the French prosecution practice traditionally based on the principle of opportunity. The French prosecutor has a broad discretion over decisions whether to prosecute or not.

The prosecution of crime is one of the responsibilities of the government, thus it is impossible to carry out its criminal policies and to make the discretion practices uniform if the government has no appropriate instruments. In France, the hierarchy and the right of the Minister of Justice to give general guidelines and individual orders are considered as such instruments.

According to the French doctrine, the prosecutor is the guardian of law, and represents the public interest as well as the interest of the government. Needless to say how contradictory these requirements might be in a politically sensitive case.

This question brings us to the status of prosecutors, which is in many respects similar to that of judges. They are both "magistrates". Until 1994, prosecutors were nominated at the proposal of the Minister of Justice by the President of the Republic. The competent authority in their disciplinary cases was also the Minister. The High Council of the Judiciary (Conseil Supérieur de la Magistrature) did not have any competence in the cases of prosecutors. Since the Constitution was amended in July 1993, the Council is now divided into a Section of Judges and a Section of Prosecutors. The latter is mainly an advisory body, but its opinion is necessary to the nomination and the disciplinary punishment of any prosecutor.

Analysis of the French system suggests that there is a tendency to provide more guarantees against the abuse of power by the Ministry and the political influence in individual cases. Furthermore, the role of the judges is preponderant in the criminal procedure. Nevertheless, politico-financial and corruption cases involving the "political class" highlighted the relationship between politics and justice so that the press often proposes to make prosecutors independent of the executive.

The German is the other great system influencing significantly the development of the Public Prosecutor's Office in Central and Eastern Europe. Though the institution was taken over from the French, nowadays there are considerable differences between the two systems.

First of all, Germany is a federal state and the prosecution of crime is mainly the responsibility of the Länder. This structure may be conceived as a counterbalance to a potential strong influence of a central prosecutorial organ, since the federal general prosecutor, who is a political official, has no right to give instructions to the prosecutor general of the Länder, who is otherwise also a political official. The federal prosecutor general as well as the federal prosecutors may be instructed by the federal Minister of Justice. The Minister of Justice of the Länder may give instructions to the prosecutors of the Länder.

Secondly, the German doctrine bluntly confesses that the Public Prosecutor Office represents the legal interest of the state, and not the public interest as in France. However, there are controversies on the interpretation of a provision of law which requires that the prosecutor general in the exercise of his function "should always be in accordance with the government's basic political convictions and aims". The question is, at least in principle, whether prosecutors should be guided by political or legal considerations. On the other hand, the office is regarded as an organ of the administration of justice and the status of the judges and prosecutors are similar.

Thirdly, the German argumentation for the external control exercised by the Minister of Justice is roughly identical with the French, but there is a very important difference. Both argue that the subordination of the office to the executive follows from the accountability of the Minister to the Parliament. The difference is that the German prosecutor has no or very little discretional power while in France this power is the main theoretical ground for the subordination to the Minister.

Fourth, the legality principle is considered not only as a guarantee against abuses of power, but also as the only principle which is in accordance with the rule of law and able to maintain public confidence. There are other guarantees, too. The judicial control is strong in the pre-trial phase, and the victim has the right to provoke prosecution when denied by the prosecutor.

Italy serves as one of the good examples for a strict separation between the public prosecution offices and the executive. In Italy, since the Constitution of 1948, public prosecutor offices are part of the Judiciary. Within the Judiciary, of course, these offices have other functions than the courts to which they are connected.

Each prosecutor (Pubblico Ministero) is a member of the Judiciary and enjoys the status of a judge. Prosecutors are appointed, affected and disciplines by the High Council of Judges (Consiglio Superiore della Magistratura). They are appointed for life and may apply for a post of judge, and vice versa. The promotion system and salary increases are automatic. All in all, the Italian prosecutor occupies a unique position among its European colleagues.

But the most striking feature of the Italian model is the lack of the hierarchical structure. No hierarchical dependence exists among the various public prosecutor offices. Each public prosecutor office is absolutely independent in performing its activities and each prosecutor enjoys a complete autonomy. Since the strong internal control and the right to give instructions and guidelines to subordinated prosecutors are missing, the civil law paradigm as opposed to common law does not apply to Italy.

In turn, Italy prosecutors have no discretionary power. The principle of legality makes it mandatory to prosecute if sufficient evidence exists to conclude that a crime has been committed. The investigation may be carried out by the police or may be conducted personally by the prosecutor. Coercive measures may be ordered by the preliminary investigation judge, except in case of urgency. Once the investigation is completed, the prosecutor submits the case to the preliminary hearing judge who decides whether the evidence is sufficient to charge the indicted person or whether the case must be dismissed immediately.

In short, the Italian prosecutors exercise their pre-trial functions under tight judicial control. At trial they act similarly to their American counterparts, since the new Italian Code of Criminal Procedure which came into force in 1989 incorporates significant adversarial elements. As for other guarantees against prosecutorial abuses or arbitrary behaviour, there exists a complex control system to prevent them.

The enormous power of the Italian prosecutor was often criticized and unsuccessful efforts have been made to curtail the sovereignty of prosecutors by trying to submit them to the direction of a general "procurator" appointed by the parliamentary majority. In fact, the executive has another way to direct the prosecution in its favour, namely by influencing the police directed by the Minister of interior.

Finally, let me say a few words about <u>an American solution</u> which is meant to enhance public confidence in justice when politically supersensitive cases occur in a system where the prosecution is the responsibility of the executive.

It follows from the United States' government system, that the Federal Attorney General (Minister of Justice) is not responsible to Congress because the Executive is the President in personam. The members of his Administration are not ministers in the European sense, since they serve at the pleasure of the President and they may be removed at any time by him. Neither the President, in his capacity of the executive, is responsible to the Congress, since he is responsible only to the people. Under federal law, federal prosecutors are answerable to the Attorney General. Thus, the Public Prosecutor Office may be very much subject to political control.

In order to keep public confidence in the impartiality of the justice, an Independent Counsel can be nominated, if there are grounds to believe that a high ranking official belonging to the executive or a person responsible for the national election campaign has committed a federal crime which is punishable with more than 6 months imprisonment.

The procedure may be initiated by a denunciation submitted by a citizen or by the Congress at the Attorney General. After a preliminary inquiry, a special court nominates an Independent Counsel and determines his mission. He is generally a jurist of merit, and must be politically uncoloured. He has powers of investigation and prosecution and obligations to report regularly to the Congress, plus the right to inform the public through the press. The most famous cases conducted by an Independent Counsel were the Nixon-Watergate and the Iran-Contra affairs.

***

What conclusion can be drawn from all this?

Firstly, there is no perfect prosecutorial system. The truth is that each system has its advantages and disadvantages. If one weight to pro and cons of the individual solutions, the arguments for one solution or another may have most to recommend them. On the other hand, there are different prosecuting systems in the West and it would be wrong to try mechanically translate a prosecuting system from one country to another.

Secondly, the social and political environment in which a new system is to be established could be regarded as crucial. I think, political as well as legal culture of a country always have to be taken into consideration when creating or modifying a system. Traditions also constitute an important factor in this respect, especially the democratic traditions. The same system could differently operate under different circumstances.

Thirdly, the constitutional and legal solutions ensuring that the functioning of the institution remains impartial and objective are of utmost importance. Such solutions may encompass either the subordination of the Public Prosecutor Office to the executive or its total independence. Of great importance is the scope of those guarantees by which the enforcement of the universal principles regarding the functioning of the Public Prosecutor's Office can be assured. Besides the legal guarantees, which are the most important, the importance of self restraint and confidence in the prosecuting authorities as well as self confidence on the government's part should be emphasized.

As I said, the question of the Public Prosecution Office's position is merely political, which means that it is decided by the actors of the political arena. This should be natural. This decision, however, can only - from a political point of view as well - be correct if it brings about a solution that gives the Public Prosecutor's Office, that is a part of the administration of justice, a chance to enjoy the confidence of the public.

All in all, I think we need a Public Prosecutor's Office that can satisfy the expectations of a democratic society and a State governed by the rule of law and meet human rights standards.

> **TOPIC 1**
>
> **THE CONSTITUTIONAL STATUS AND THE INTERNAL STRUCTURE OF THE PUBLIC PROSECUTION IN A STATE GOVERNED BY THE RULE OF LAW**
>
> by
>
> **José Manuel SANTOS PAIS**
> **Public Prosecutor (Portugal)**

Presentation of Topic 1
in its Pan-European context

## 1. Introduction

From the European-wide perspective, there is a major basic difficulty in speaking of a Prosecutor General's Department or Office and the persons who together make up the State Prosecution Service. The entity varies greatly from one Western European country to another and its various versions may well have little in common, apart from the name, which itself does not cover the same principles, philosophy, structure or organisation.

Above all, the Prosecution Service reflects the unique historical evolution of each country and legal system, and its development is closely linked to unfolding changes in criminal procedures in recent years.

## 2. Historical evolution of the State Prosecution Service

By and large, it can be said that the institution of State Prosecution Service exists in two main organisational forms: the continental systems, which are directly or indirectly based on the Napoleonic model, and the common law systems. In most cases, different approaches are used to meet identical needs. The point which the two systems sometimes have in common is the proximity of the executive power.

The issues posed in this field are often common to the two systems. For example, is the Prosecution Service an administrative body (as in Germany) or a judicial body (Belgium, Portugal)? Does it form part of the executive (Germany, Belgium, France) or the judiciary (Spain, Portugal)? Although considered to be part of the executive power, can the Prosecution Service be regarded as part of the judiciary (Germany, Belgium, France)? Is it a genuine judicial body on a par with the Bench

(Belgium, France, Portugal) or not (Spain)[1]? Must it defend the government's interests, the public interest or the law?

## 3. The impact of human rights on judicial organisation

**3.1** In recent times, particularly since the adoption of the Universal Declaration of Human Rights, there have been profound changes in legal systems, especially in the organisation and powers of judges and the Prosecution Service and in judicial organisation in general. New concepts of an extraordinary scope have been introduced in such important texts as the European Convention on Human Rights and the United Nations International Covenant on Civil and Political Rights, for example the concepts of an independent and impartial tribunal, of legal authority (Art. 5 (1) c of the ECHR) and of officer authorised by law to exercise judicial power (Art. 5 (3) of the ECHR).

**3.2** In addition to provisions in conventions, other principles concerning the system of the administration of justice have been set forth in numerous declarations and other texts, including:

- Basic principles on the independence of the judiciary (VIIth UN Congress on the prevention of crime) and Procedures for the effective implementation of those principles (ECOSOC Resolution 1989/60);

- Guidelines on the role of prosecutors (VIIth UN Congress on the prevention of crime).

## 4. The State Prosecution Service: giving fresh impetus to its role in modern society

**4.1** It would appear that the concerns of the legislator and the public at large have shifted away from the structure and operations of the courts and that their attention is now focusing on the Prosecution Service. A far-reaching discussion is presently under way on the special problems of the prosecuting authorities, in particular with regard to their basic nature, their role in proceedings, the scope of their functions and their real independence *vis-à-vis* the executive power.

The impact of this discussion can be seen in the fact that legislators in a number of countries[2] have turned to the question in recent years and have:

- drafted new institutional acts on the Prosecution Service;
- consolidated its role, sometimes even at constitutional level;
- broadened its powers in the area of criminal procedure;
- recognised its importance in international legal co-operation, notably in criminal law.

---

[1] In Italy, the State Counsel's Office and the judiciary form part of the same career.

[2] In Portugal, for example.

## 5. Constitutional status of the Prosecution Service

### 5.1 Appointing the Prosecutor General and members of the Prosecution Service

The rules also differ from one European country to another with regard to selecting the Prosecutor General and the members of the Prosecution Service. This choice may fall to:

- the Head of State: the President of the Republic or the King (Belgium, Bulgaria, France[3]), sometimes at the proposal of the Prime Minister (as in Portugal[4]), the Council of Ministers (as in Spain[5]), the Parliament (as in Slovakia) or specialised councils (as in Romania);

- the Parliament (United Kingdom, Hungary, Macedonia), sometimes at the proposal of other bodies (for example the President of the Republic, as in Moldavia);

- the government[6], in particular through the intermediary of the Council of Ministers (Greece) or the Minister of Justice (Germany, France, Netherlands);

- special bodies, such as the Judicial Service Commission (Italy, Croatia) or the Prosecution Service Commission (Portugal[7])[8].

### 5.2 Political responsibility of the Prosecutor General

Needless to say, the political responsibility of the Prosecutor General is closely linked to the way in which the post is filled, a task which may, in particular, fall to:

---

[3] The members of the Prosecution Service are appointed by decree by the President after simple notification of the Judicial Service Commission. The Chief Prosecutors of the Court of Cassation and the Courts of Appeal are appointed by the Minister of Justice.

[4] This concerns the appointment of the Prosecutor General.

[5] With the concurrence of the General Council of the judicial power.

[6] In certain countries, the Prosecutor (Attorney) General is a member of the executive (United States of America, United Kingdom, Poland).

[7] This concerns the appointment of members of the Prosecution Service, with the exception of the Prosecutor General.

[8] There are also other selection methods. For example, the Prosecutor General of the Russian Federation is appointed and dismissed by the Council of the Federation, at the proposal of the President of the Federation.

- the Parliament (Albania, Belarus, Hungary, Slovakia, Macedonia);
- the government (Germany, Belgium, France, Czech Republic);
- the President of the Republic and the Prime Minister[9].

## 5.3 Political responsibility and term of office of the Prosecutor General

The political responsibility of the Prosecutor General and his/her term of office are also subtly related. It could be argued that one of the best ways to ensure the independence of the Prosecutor General would be through a predefined term of office, during which the he/she would enjoy full independence *vis-à-vis* the other State powers.

In some cases, the Prosecutor General would thus be appointed for an indefinite period, remaining in office as long as he/she enjoys the confidence of the appointing body or bodies, and in other cases would have a fixed term of office.

Such arguments must be taken with a grain of salt. An appointment for an indefinite period is not necessarily prejudicial to the independence of the office. It is sufficient to ensure independence through appropriate means, such as by requiring for the appointment that action to be taken by several bodies (as in Portugal) or by defining regulations to prevent outside interference.

A similar line of reasoning might be advanced for fixed-term appointments. This system can coexist with possible interference and lead to situations in which the Prosecutor General, having demonstrated excessive independence, is not reappointed.

## 5.4 Relations with other State bodies: prevention of improper interference

Whatever the system, the fundamental principle that must be upheld is that of preventing any improper interference by other State bodies. This does not necessarily mean that the Prosecution Service is completely independent of these other bodies, but that its relations with them are subject to specific and public rules and are open to democratic scrutiny. In democracy, there can be no power without responsibility.

## 5.5 Relations with the judiciary

Given the interrelated nature of their work in the system of the administration of justice, special relations must be established between the Prosecution Service and the judiciary.

There are several ways to co-ordinate their activities:

---

[9] This is the case in Portugal, where the Prosecutor General remains in office as long as he/she enjoys the confidence of the President of the Republic and the Prime Minister.

- the Prosecution Service and the judiciary form a sole body, whose members may be assigned to duties with one service or the other (France, Italy);

- the Prosecution Service is an independent service but part of the judiciary (Portugal);

- the Prosecution Service is an independent body that performs judicial functions, but is not necessarily part of the judiciary (Belgium).

**6.    The function of the Prosecution Service: unlimited growth?**

In general, the duties of the Prosecution Service have grown in recent years[10], gradually covering several new fields, of which examples are given below from different judicial systems, classed by specific area of activity:

**6.1    Criminal law**: instituting criminal proceedings, conducting criminal investigations (even if these are actually carried out by other bodies), promoting and collaborating in crime prevention, monitoring the police etc.

**6.2    Social sphere**: defending the social rights of workers and their families.

**6.3    Civil law**: representing the State, the autonomous regions, the local authorities, those lacking legal capacity, persons uncertain and persons whose whereabouts are unknown; taking action in cases of bankruptcy and insolvency.

**6.4    Ensuring due process**:

- defending the independence of the courts in the framework of their jurisdiction and ensuring that the courts discharge their duties in accordance with the Constitution and the law;

- pursuing the execution of court decisions so as to ensure their authority;

- appealing against decisions based on collusion between the parties with the intention of evading the law or pronounced in actual violation of the law.

**6.5    Constitutional law**: monitoring the constitutionality of legislative measures.

**6.6    Administrative law**: monitoring the legality of administrative measures, drafting legal opinions at the request of the government (through the legal advisers to the various ministries or a Consultative Council working within the Prosecutor General's Office).

---

[10]    The examples of several legal systems in Central and Eastern Europe suggest the opposite trend (reduction in the duties of the State Prosecution Service), almost certainly the result of the profound changes experienced by the "Prokuraturas" in most recent years and the efforts of these countries to meet the conditions for a State governed by the rule of law.

**6.7** **Environmental protection law**: protection of the interests of the population endangered by pollution or other acts affecting the environment.

**6.8** **Consumer protection**: protection of consumers against various economic operators.

**6.9** **Legislative reform**:

- submission to the government or Parliament of proposed legislative measures to improve the effectiveness of the Prosecution Service and judicial institutions;

- submission of information to Parliament or the government on omissions, shortcomings or contradictions in legal texts;

- drafting of proposals to the government on legislative measures to make constitutional provisions enforceable.

**6.10** **International co-operation**: increasing activities in the area of extradition, mutual assistance in criminal matters etc.

**7.** **The structure of the Prosecution Service: consequence of its duties?**

**7.1** **Structural and organisational models**

There are several structural and organisational models for the Prosecution Service in Europe, including:

- a classical centralised, hierarchial model, headed by the Prosecutor General (Spain, Portugal), in which the latter, together with the senior members of the Prosecution Service, have the power to give instructions to persons under their orders;

- a decentralised, locally co-ordinated model (Italy) in which, strictly speaking, there are no co-ordinating links between the members of the Prosecution Service in the various courts;

- a decentralised model with co-ordination by a group of Chief Prosecutors mainly attached to the various appeal courts (Germany, Belgium, France), which are effectively in charge of the members of the Prosecution Service in courts under the jurisdiction of those same appeal courts, the Chief Prosecutor to the Court of Cassation being unable to intervene in the activities of the other members of the Prosecution Service.

## 7.2 Adaptation of the model to the legal and/or administrative structure of the country

In many European countries, the Prosecution Service is modelled on the legal and/or administrative structure of the country concerned: the administrative districts are usually the same as the judicial districts, the appointment of members of the Prosecution Service to the various courts (Supreme Court, Courts of Appeal, courts of first instance) generally being made as a function of seniority and career advancement, as well as of the status of the court concerned.

## 7.3 Chain of command

The chain of command is a principle whose main purpose is to ensure that the Prosecution Service is consistent in its actions. This is of particular importance from the point of view of equal treatment of all citizens before the law.

But this principle also raises difficult issues: how far should following the orders of superiors go? What restrictions should senior members of the Prosecution Service or other State bodies be allowed to impose on the freedom of opinion of their subordinates, particularly with regard to proceedings?

In this area, regardless of the solutions actually adopted (see below §§ 8 and 9), it is necessary above all to demonstrate a concern for achieving a transparent judicial system, in particular by accepting the basic monitoring role of citizens, who are the ones who use the system of the administration of justice, of the media and of other members of the legal professions. As stated earlier, in democracy there can be no power without responsibility (see above, 5.4).

## 8. The autonomy of the Prosecution Service *vis-à-vis* other State bodies: a problem with no solution or a solution with no problems?

**8.1** The nature and limits of relations between the Prosecution Service and the executive power is probably the most difficult problem that the legislator in each country must deal with in its relevant legislation.

**8.2** The arguments in favour of the different options in this area are well known:

- Placing the Prosecution Service, to varying degrees, under the authority of the executive, which flows from the latter's political responsibility before the Parliament for all matters concerning the system of the administration of justice. The question is how to ensure this responsibility in actual fact if the executive, and the Ministry of Justice in particular, is deprived of this power of control, which can take several forms: the power to give instructions of a general nature or in a specific case, disciplinary power over the members of the Prosecution Service, the power to appoint, transfer and dismiss these members etc.

- Providing for the independence of the Prosecution Service *vis-à-vis* the executive, without prejudice to the relations that must necessarily exist between the power that usually is in charge of defining policy in the area of the administration of justice and one of the bodies (the Prosecution Service) best placed to monitor its implementation.

In addition to these two options, there are intermediate possibilities that allow for varying degrees of autonomy for the Prosecution Service *vis-à-vis* the executive power.

**8.3** The case of Portugal is very interesting in this regard, because the Constitution itself states that the superior body of the Prosecution Service is the Prosecutor General's Office and not the government; this ensures that the Prosecution Service is not subordinate to the government.

Thus, the Prosecution Service is doubly independent, particularly for matters concerning criminal procedure[11]: it is independent of the executive (principle of the non-interference of the latter in this area) and independent of the judiciary, in that the Prosecution Service is conceived as a judicial body separate from and parallel to the Bench.

**8.4** The relations between the Prosecution Service and the executive in Portugal are specifically defined in the Institutional Act on the State Prosecution Service. For example, under Article 59 of this Act, the Minister of Justice can:

a. convey to the Prosecutor General specific instructions concerning civil actions in which the State is an interested party;

b. authorise the Prosecution Service, once the supervising government body has been heard, to hear, settle or discontinue civil actions in which the State is a party;

c. request, through the intermediary of the Prosecutor General, service reports or information from any judge or staff member of the Prosecution Service;

d. request from the Prosecution Service Commission such information and clarifications and make such communications to this body as it deems fit;

e. ask the Prosecutor General to conduct inspections, investigations or inquiries, in particular of police bodies.

The law also stipulates that the Minister of Justice may attend meetings of the Prosecution Service Commission when this is judged appropriate, in order to make communications and to seek or provide information (Section 29 of the Act on the State Prosecution Service).

---

[11] The fact that it represents the State in civil matters naturally means that the Service is not (in its role as State Counsel) independent of the executive in this area also. See below 8.4 and 8.5.

**8.5** Consequently, the Minister of Justice may give specific instructions to the Prosecution Service in matters concerning civil proceedings when the latter is representing the State and may authorise it to hear, settle or discontinue in this area, just as a client might do with legal counsel.

On the other hand, in the area of criminal procedure, the Minister of Justice has no power to give instructions to the Prosecutor General or to members of the Prosecution Service, apart from the request, through the intermediary of the Prosecutor General, for service reports and information, for an opportunity to make communications before the Prosecution Service Commission or for information and clarifications from it or, in general, for the Prosecutor General to conduct inspections, investigations and inquiries, in particular of police bodies.

## 9. Supervising the activities of the State Prosecution Service

**9.1** Although the problem of the independence of the Prosecution Service is of particular importance in today's modern societies, that does not mean that in those countries in which subordination to the executive power is greater that certain segments of this body cannot enjoy, in discharging their duties, the necessary conditions for defending the public interest and ensuring full respect of the law.

The problem of the independence of the Prosecution Service cannot be considered in isolation, but only in conjunction with other questions, such as the type and effectiveness of the means of defence and the activities of the service with regard to what may be improper orders from other State bodies, the aim being to ensure respect for the principle of legality, as well as the impartiality and objectivity that must constitute the essential features of its activity.

**9.2** Respect for these characteristics presupposes, in particular:

- the complete absence of any improper interference, notably of a political nature, in its work;

- that the members of the Prosecution Service must only obey orders, directives and instructions that are legal and that have been given in accordance with the law, respect for human rights and the interests that the service must safeguard.

**9.3** Once again, Portuguese law has an interesting arrangement in this regard. The duty of the members of the Prosecution Service to obey orders is not unconditional, even within its own hierarchy, as is the case with the military hierarchy, nor is it confined, as in the civil service, to the basic duty to refuse illegal orders or to "respectful protest".

To deal with this genuine judicial service, the legislators have sought ways to enable its members to act with full inner freedom.

It is for this reason that, under Section 58 of the Act on the State Prosecution Service, members of the service must refuse to carry out illegal directives, orders and instructions and may do so on the basis of a grave violation of their legal conscience.

This refusal must be in writing and must be preceded by a personal presentation of the reasons invoked.

In the event of such a refusal, the official who gave the directive, order or instruction may discontinue institute proceedings or ask another subordinate to carry out that directive, order or instruction.

**9.4** The right to refuse is not, however, unlimited. The legislators have conceived it as a last resort for the conscience of the person who receives the order and have placed strict conditions on it, which protect the essential sense of the State Prosecution Service as a hierarchal service and as such naturally subordinate to the policy of the Prosecutor General or the Prosecution Service Commission.

The following cannot be refused under the above law:

a. decisions taken by a superior under the Code of Procedure;

b. directives, orders and instructions given by the Prosecutor General, except on grounds of illegality.

In the first case, the point is to respect the procedural provisions themselves by giving precedence to the decisions of the superior body over those of the subordinate one. In the second case, given that the decision of the Prosecutor General, as the highest official in the State Prosecution Service, is a decision of last resort, it was deemed necessary to restrict the possibility of refusal to the sole case of illegality.

**9.5** Lastly, with regard to disciplinary action, Section 24 of the Act on the State Prosecution Service stipulates that the Prosecution Service Commission is alone empowered to:

a. appoint, assign, transfer, promote, discuss and evaluate professional merit, as well as to take disciplinary action and, in general, to carry out all similar acts concerning members of the State Prosecution Service, with the exception of the Prosecutor General;

...

g. propose the annual inspection plan, inspections and inquiries.

**10.** **Advantages of the new democratic societies in the field of democratic reform**

**10.1** In view of the interests involved, the problems affecting the system of the administration of justice are particularly difficult. It therefore seems fully natural that in general, reforms in this area should be carried out cautiously and gradually so as to find solutions that will gain the support of the members of the various legal professions, as well as of the public and the political forces represented in the Parliament of each country. It is also important to ensure that these reforms have sufficient time to take shape so that they can be properly assessed and, where necessary, amended or even discarded.

In this context, it is clear that far-reaching institutional change, particularly at constitutional level, sometimes enables rapid and profound reforms to be achieved which otherwise would be impossible under the normal working of the judicial system and would take decades to be fully implemented.

**10.2** Portugal is a case in point. Having thoroughly reformed its system for the protection of fundamental rights at constitutional level in 1976 with the approval of a new and thoroughly democratic Constitution, the implications of this change made themselves felt in all areas of judicial activity, for example with regard to the status of judges and prosecutors, criminal and civil procedure, access to the courts and to avenues of redress for violations of individual rights, judicial organisation etc.

**10.3** Moreover, all these changes had to be carried out in a relatively short period, either as the result of new constitutional or legislative provisions or following admission to new international bodies, notably the Council of Europe, after which the domestic legal system was brought into line with international standards providing greater protection than those in existence in the country, above all through the ratification of such international instruments as the European Convention on Human Rights and the United Nations International Covenant on Civil and Political Rights.

**10.4** Once it became possible to benefit from the experience of other countries or of international organisations (the Council of Europe, United Nations etc), the Portuguese legislative reform commissions set up in the judicial and procedural fields and in the entire area of the protection of human rights had available, virtually over night, a vitally important body of information on applicable international provisions (conventions, resolutions, recommendations, declarations etc) on subjects that they needed to address, as well as the relevant legal texts of several other countries.

It is understandable that this greatly facilitated their task and enabled them to complete their work much more expeditiously.

**10.5** But despite all the assistance provided, experience remains essential for assessing the reforms undertaken. The information on international and comparative law is enormously useful, but each country has its own unique features which must be taken into consideration whenever a change is made in the system of the administration of justice.

The authorities of each country, even if in close collaboration with international bodies, are in the best position to assess the results of the reforms undertaken in their judicial systems.

## 11. The State Prosecution Service: organisation or corps of judicial officers?

### 11.1 The role of the Prosecutor General

In countries in which the Prosecutor General is in charge of the State Prosecution Service, the role is an important one.

This is why there is such concern about how the post is filled and how to define the Prosecutor General's responsibilities and the body of which he/she is the head.

Consequently, in these countries the Prosecutor General has a special status because of the responsibilities and tasks attached to the post within the system of the administration of justice. Reason enough to ensure that the person chosen for the position enjoys sufficient prestige to discharge his/her duties with distinction and integrity.

**11.2** It must be borne in mind, however, that the Prosecutor General is not the only official in the State Prosecution Service. The activities of its other members are equally important for its prestige. The role of these other officials, their effectiveness and their public image, like that of the Prosecutor General, are an indispensable condition for their acceptance by citizens, the beneficiaries of the system of justice.

Although it is certainly very important to devise and draft good legislation, if the members of the service are not adequately prepared for the performance of their duties, legislation will at most be a mere expression of good intentions, with no actual link to judicial reality.

## 12. The vital role of information and training for the State Prosecution Service

**12.1** This brings us to the last part of this presentation: the importance for the members of the State Prosecution Service of information, initial training, for example by a national training school, and later in-service training.

Information and training are indispensable for the application of new legislation, especially when it aims to ensure better protection of the individual human rights and an opening-up to other judicial systems and norms, in particular through international instruments applicable in domestic law.

**12.2** Such information and training can also help the State Prosecution Service prepare for a growing range of responsibilities that come with new developments in modern society: the need to take rapid and effective action against national and transnational crime and to combat particularly serious threats to democracy (violent crime, economic crime etc).

**12.3** This cannot be done efficiently without adequate information and training, especially in the area of international co-operation, where the members of the national legal service must be adequately trained to understand the judicial realities in other countries and the specific problems posed by the relevant international instruments in force.

## Conclusions

**I.  The constitutional status of the State Prosecution Service in a democratic State governed by the rule of law**

**1.** The constitutional status of the State Prosecution Service must be defined within the framework of the requirements of a democratic society: the rule of law, pluralist political democracy, free elections and the protection of human rights.

**2.** The Constitution should define the status of the Prosecutor General and of his/her Office, as well as that of the State Prosecution Service with regard to the overall structure of the State and its bodies in order to avoid any ambiguity in this area.

**3.** The Constitution, or the law, should also define the nature and limits of relations between the State Prosecution Service and other State bodies (notably the parliament, the government, the judiciary etc) in respect of its functional autonomy and the rule of law.

**4.** The Prosecutor General's and the Prosecution Service should be regarded as essential parts of the system of the administration of justice of every State, along with the judiciary and the bar.

**II.  The structure of the State Prosecution Service and the principles governing its activities**

**5.** The organisation of the Prosecutor General Office and the Prosecution Service must take into consideration the social and political situation of the State concerned, as well as its democratic and legal traditions of respect for the rule of law and democracy.

**6.** It must also take into account the judicial and/or administrative structure of the State.

**7.** The structure of the State Prosecution Service must be tailored to the type of tasks and responsibilities that it is called upon to discharge.

**8.** In performing those tasks, members of the Prosecution Service must always strive to remain impartial and objective. Any decision to make prosecutors subordinate to the officials or bodies should take these requirements into account, as well as the fact that they should be accountable only to the law and hence free from any improper influence, particularly political, and should ensure protection of human rights without discrimination.

**9.** Without prejudice to the need to maintain consistency in their activities, the members of the State Prosecution Service must enjoy a degree of autonomy at local and intermediate level in order to ensure that justice remains close to its beneficiaries.

**10.** In performing their function, the members of the State Prosecution Service must remember that they perform a social function of the utmost importance within the system of the administration of justice and that they are accountable for their actions to their compatriots.

**11.** The members of the State Prosecution Service should have access to adequate information and training to perform their duties properly, particularly in the fields of the protection of human rights and international legal co-operation.

# TOPIC 1

## THE CONSTITUTIONAL STATUS AND THE INTERNAL STRUCTURE OF THE PUBLIC PROSECUTION IN A STATE GOVERNED BY THE RULE OF LAW

by

**Attila HLAVATHY**
Director of the Secretariat
Prosecutor General's Office of the Republic of Hungary

**General Presentation of the solutions
of Central and Eastern European countries**

drafted on the basis of the answers to the Questionnaire of the Council of Europe received from the following countries (in alphabetical order):

    Albania
    Belarus
    Bulgaria
    Croatia
    Macedonia (Former Yugoslav Republic of)
    Poland
    Romania
    Russian Federation
    Slovak Republic
    Slovenia

# THE CONSTITUTIONAL STATUS AND THE INTERNAL STRUCTURE OF THE PUBLIC PROSECUTION

## I.

1.     As the first regional rapporteur, I am in a favourable and unfavourable situation at the same time. I am in a favourable situation on the one hand because I have the chance to firstly throw light on how useful even the preparation of such a multilateral conference may be, first of all in terms of producing highly valuable comparative material on generalizing and typifying the potential development tendencies. But the success had a main condition: the effective support by the Council of Europe morally, politically, intellectually and financially.

I would like to take the opportunity to express my personal thanks to the representatives of the Directorate of Legal Affairs primarily because they have supported and continue to support this meeting. Its idea was raised also by the Hungarian representatives during and after the conference organized in Vienna last May. The activity of the Hungarian representatives has not decreased, moreover, it has become even more intensive: Mr. Endre Bócz, the Prosecutor General of Budapest, is not only the regional rapporteur on topic 3, but at the same time the General Rapporteur of the entire conference, as well. As far as I am concerned, besides being regional rapporteur I have been trying to coordinate from Hungarian side the preparations and the course of the conference.

2.     On the other hand, my situation is somewhat unfavourable, because before the discussion of substantial issues, it is my task to refer to those technical questions which do touch the other regional reports and rapporteurs, respectively.

In my view, the following issues have to be raised by all means: We hope to receive all the answers to the Questionnaire until the end of the summer the latest, from all the invited countries, to be able to pay attention to the solutions of all the states concerned when drafting the regional reports. It has not happened, answers were received - as I have indicated on the first page of the written report - from ten countries (no answer was received from the following countries: the Czech Republic, Estonia, Latvia, Lithuania, Moldova and Ukraine).

In spite of the lack of the answers to the Questionnaire, we had some information on the Prosecution of the Czech Republic and the Ukraine as a result of the bilateral relations, the conference held in Vienna last year, and the partial monitoring of foreign legislation. We hope, their solutions will also be *mutatis mutandis* reflected in the regional reports. On the other hand, we are much more uncertain than informed about the position of the Prosecution of the Baltic states and Moldova, therefore, their solutions could not even indirectly be considered.

The most excellent chance to attain the appropriate information is offered by this conference. I am convinced that we shall mutually receive the appropriate information from each other, and may leave this conference with realistic and comprehensive views about what "Prokuratura" is today in the Central and Eastern European countries, what prospects of development they have, and transformation of what nature is necessitated and possible.

Another general question is what method was applied in the treatment of the answers to the Questionnaire. The fact by itself that my topic, consequently my regional report is the first one does not involve, that the method I have applied should be taken as a guideline.

The rapporteurs have themselves decided what method to apply on the basis of the nature of the topic, and the quantity and quality of information respectively, therefore differences may occur in the approaches and concepts applied in the regional reports.

On my behalf, the starting point was, that the Questionnaire actually represents a certain summary of themes, and the main objective was not making an inventory sort of composition or a statistical comparison. Typifying the major tendencies, the introduced solutions and the ones planned to be introduced is much more important, and also doing this with the intention to discuss the potentional advantages and disadvantages with the participants as colleagues.

## II.

1. Before discussing in detail our topic, the constitutional position of the Public Prosecution and its internal structure, I wish to emphasize the following:

I owe a debt of thanks to the author of the introductory lecture, to Mr. Kálmán Györgyi, the Prosecutor General of the Republic of Hungary for making my task - and the task of all of us, I think - easier. For he has described the political, social and legal background, and the major model potentials that should be primarily considered regarding the present position and transformational possibilities of the Prosecution in the former socialist countries and their successor states. By doing so, he has helped regional presentations - and perhaps also the comments of the national representatives - to basically concentrate on professional issues.

As the first regional rapporteur, I take this opportunity at once.

2. As I have mentioned, the Questionnaire should be primarily considered as a summary of themes. It involves that certain questions are often interwoven or overlapping, or represent different approaches to the same problem not only within the individual chapter, but sometimes even between chapters. This is often reflected in the answers given to the Questionnaire, when at certain question instead of repeating one refers to answers formulated with preceding questions.

Considering all these, in the treatment of the themes of chapter I and II of the Questionnaire, I do not follow a strict internal division, instead I try to place the stress on the interrelations. By doing so, I will avoid referring to the individual points of the Questionnaire.

3.  The most feasible way for treating the position of the Public Prosecution in the constitutional structure is to do it within the framework of the classical category of the division of power branches (the separation of powers) - and this is what most of the national reports have done.

The trichotomy of the separation of powers, that is, the division of power into the Legislative, Executive and Judiciary, has long been disputed from sociological and politological viewpoint - and not without any reason.

Just an example: local self-governments often represent a serious check and counter-balance against the central government, and even against the Parliament, especially when the local self-governments are dominated by the opposition.

Another example: the Constitutional Court, established in most of the countries of our region, may become an almost entirely independent branch of the power, especially if it has the power within its own competence to annul any act of Parliament or any of its provisions. Just to mention two Hungarian facts: death penalty was annulled not by the Parliament, but it was the Constitutional Court that qualified it as unconstitutional; therefore the role of the Legislation was limited to the implementation of the Constitutional Court decision. Another decision is directly related to the sphere of responsibility and competences of the Prokuratura: early this year, the Constitutional Court declared the right of the prosecutor to initiate civil litigation on public interest, or to appear in cases under process between two other parties also as anticonstitutional. On the basis of the idea and practice of the "Ministère Public" as model for the continental public prosecution systems, it would be rather difficult to explain the rationale of this decision to the foreign colleagues. I abandon the attempt of explanation not only for the sake of saving time, but also because this decision is even for the majority of the Hungarian legal experts - including me - hardly understandable.

4.  I have made this little detour in order to show that the position of the Public Prosecution in the constitutional structure could be studied not only in the framework of the Montesquieu division and in the interrelation of its elements. On my part, I would be delighted to see that the discussion exceeds this strict trichotomy. Since the Questionnaire, due to practical reasons, inquired only about the relation to the Executive and the Judiciary, the answers were also concentrating on these relations, consequently, I will limit the sphere of study in this sense.

Regarding its relation to the Parliament, a common characteristic of the Prokuratura of this region was, that - though the person of the Procurator General - the Prokuratura was attached to the supreme state organ. The Prosecutor General was accountable to this organ -that had a different name at different places, but similar competences -, and it was again this organ that had the power to decide on his election or appointment, moreover, on his release, or to initiate all these acts at the President of the Republic. The only serious exception to this principal rule was represented by Poland where the Prokuratura was never subordinated to the Parliament. The Constitution of 1952 subordinated the Prosecution to the Council of State: the Prosecutor General was appointed and released by the Council of State, and was obliged to report on his activity to the Council with annual regularity. This situation existed until April 1989. Probably these antecedents, namely the lack of subordination to the Parliament also played a role in Poland's choosing an entirely different solution than the other countries. Later I will return to some details of this question.

5. The reform of public law, in some form, has been started in all the countries of the region, but the impact of this process on the constitutional position of the Prokuratura was of different extent and direction.

The present and planned constitutional position of the Prokuratura within our region may be typified as follows:

A. Maintenance of the subordination to the Parliament in an unchanged form, or with certain minor changes. This category includes Russia, Belarus, Slovakia, Ukraine (on the basis of information attained at the conference in Vienna, May 1993), Macedonia, and under the law in force, Hungary as well.

B. The Public Prosecution is approached to the Executive in Romania, Slovenia and the Czech Republic (on the basis of information attained on relevant legal regulation) without integrating it into the Executive as it happened in Poland.

C. One tries to approach the Prokuratura to the Judiciary or to include it in the scope of this power in Albania, Bulgaria and Croatia.

Although no answers have been received from 6 countries until the closure of the manuscript of the regional report, the constitutional solutions or planned transformations in these countries may presumably be well fitted into one of the above described types.

6. Approaching the Prokuratura to the Executive in the countries concerned essentially means that the rights and powers connected with the supervision and control of the Prosecution are divided between the Prosecutor General and the Minister of Justice.

In the Romanian regulation this basically means that the operative control of the work of the Prokuratura is exerted by the Prosecutor General's Office by the Supreme Court. This Office is in command of an appropriate apparatus, having, within its framework e.g. a department of criminal prosecution and criminalistics, as well as a department for control organization and scientific matters. The head of this Office is the Prosecutor General who has all supervisory and control powers and competences over all the prosecution offices. The Prosecutor General has the power to give instructions, even directly, to all subordinated prosecutors, although instruction is normally given by line of command through the head of the territorial prosecution office, the so-called first prosecutor.

At the same time, the Minister of Justice exerts a "mixed" type of supervision, where the elements of the external and internal supervision are mingled. The Minister has the right to require the Prosecutor General to give a report on the work of the prosecution offices, and may give him guidelines on the fight against crime. It is the Minister, who has the right to decide - upon the recommendation of the Prosecutor General - on the establishing of prosecution agencies, the structure of these agencies, furthermore, he has the right to appoint all prosecutors, to decide on issues related to the promotion and assignment of the prosecutors, and may initiate disciplinary proceedings - besides the Prosecutor General - against the prosecutors. In exercising his supervisory rights, the Minister is assisted by the so-called "prosecutor inspectors" working at the Office of the Prosecutor General by the Supreme Court, and at the prosecution offices by the higher courts.

The Minister has the right to give instruction to the competent prosecutor in individual cases, but only in writing and through the Prosecutor General. The instruction can be only of positive nature, that is, it may refer to the initiation or further continuation of the proceedings, but may never order to stop criminal proceedings once legally started.

In accordance with the Slovene regulation in force, the Prokuratura is a so-called "independent state organ", which has an obligation of reporting on its work and on the state of legality to the Parliament. The enactment of a new law on the "State Prosecution Office", however, is on its way, and will presumably enter into effect on 1st January 1995. The bill is going to give a greater scope of competence to the agencies of the Executive, primarily, to the Ministry of Justice. In the sense of the bill, the Prosecutor General regulates the structure and operation of the Prosecution in agreement with the Minister of Justice, and supervises the internal activity of the Prosecution again in conjunction with the Minister. The Minister may require report on the state of individual cases, and the prosecution offices - beyond continuing to prepare an annual report for the Parliament - will be obliged to prepare reports for the Ministry of Justice as well.

The internal structure of the Prosecution in Slovenia follows the "classical" Central and Eastern European model, and the new bills do not intend to change this. That is, the scope of competences of the Office of the Prosecutor General of Slovenia extends to the entire republic, the competences of the higher public prosecution offices shall be adjusted to the competences of the high courts, and those of the district offices to the competences of the district courts.

On the basis of the information gained through the bilateral relations and the legal regulation, the Prosecution of the Czech Republic has also preserved the same division of structure, where the top agency of the apparatus is the Office of the Prosecutor General, and not the Ministry of Justice.

Although the entire organization was given a new name - the traditional "Prokuratura" was replace by "Statni zastupitelstvi", - meaning state representation, the operative control as a whole was not fully integrated into the structure of the Ministry of Justice.

7.      The inclusion of the Prokuratura in the scope of the Judiciary was most consistently implemented in Bulgaria. In the sense of the new Constitution of the Republic of Bulgaria passed in 1991, the Prosecution is a part of the Judiciary, and since the Judiciary is independent of the Legislative and Executive, this independence is also true for the Prokuratura. The Bulgarian report follows the process of becoming independent step by step and draws the following conclusions: the unified and centralized Prokuratura was established by the constitutions of the year 1947 and of 1971, with this making a significant advance in the direction of separating the Prokuratura from the Executive. This process was completed by the Constitution of 1991: the Prosecutor General is no longer elected by and responsible to the Parliament, thus the Prokuratura is no longer subordinated to the Legislative either.

This achievement, i.e. that the Prosecutor General and the prosecutors have become independent not only of the Executive, but also of the Legislative was made possible by the Act on the Supreme Council of the Judiciary in 1991. The Supreme Council is a body of the Judiciary, that has the right to appoint, promote, demote in rank and remove judges and prosecutors, and to make proposals of this kind, respectively. Therefore, substantial changes have been made compared to the former situation. The most spectacular of all these changes was the fact that the Prosecutor General is no longer elected by the Parliament for a term of five years, but it is the President of the Republic, who appoints - upon the recommendation of the Supreme Council - the Prosecutor General for a term of seven years, while the appointment of the other prosecutors is a direct competence of the Supreme Council.

Croatia follows a similar solution - both in its nature and essentially. In accordance with the Constitution of 1990, the Prokuratura is part of the Judiciary, the judges and the prosecutors are appointed and released by the Supreme Council of Justice of the Republic, but the competence regarding decisions on disciplinary responsibility also belongs to the Supreme Council. In the meantime, a new law is being prepared on the Prosecution, and the draft bill is open to public debate. The bill - in accordance with the Constitution - provides that the Prosecution is independent both of the government and the Parliament; all the prosecutors are appointed by the Supreme Council of Justice of the Republic, within this, the Prosecutor General, and the prosecutors at higher level for a term of 8 years, and the other prosecutors for an undefined period of time.

Considering the answers given to the Questionnaire, the regulation in Albania seems to be eclectic. Although the Prokuratura is part of the Judiciary, the Prosecutor General is elected by the Parliament. The report from Albania gives the impression that this process of reform may be lengthened for a long time, and not even the direction of the reform has been ultimately decided.

One option is to subordinate the Prokuratura to the Ministry of Justice, while another alternative suggests retaining the prosecution as a part of the Judiciary, and again there are many who would prefer to have some kind of mixed system.

8.     The Polish solution has to be mentioned separately. As we have said, the Polish Prokuratura has never been subordinated to the Parliament. Between July 1952 and April 1989 it was supervised by the State Council, and because of the liquidation of the State Council as institution, it was drawn under the supervision of the President of the Republic for a couple of months. Then the amendment of the Constitution in December 1989 produced something so special that even in this region of ours, where we are so much used to legal experimenting it should be considered a unique: namely, the Office of the Public Prosecutor, as a supreme agency, was simply ceased, and incorporated into the Ministry of Justice, and the function of the Minister of Justice and that of the Prosecutor General were fused. At the liquidation of the Prokuratura Generalna, not even a special prosecutor's division was considered necessary to be maintained or established to proceed in cases before the supreme Court, that could exercise the functions of the French "Parquet Général de la Cour de Cassation", or of the Austrian "Generalprokuratur". For the professional control of the prosecution and to carry out the "classical" tasks of a Prosecutor General's Office of our region they have created a department, called Department of Prosecution (Departament Prokuratury) in the Ministry of Justice.

Since the Polish report explains neither the theoretical rationale of this solution, nor the evaluation of the practical experiences, as a regional rapporteur, I do not feel entitled to go into a more profound explanation. One comment, however, seems to be correct and justified by all means, namely, that the Polish solution in effect is unfamiliar with both the former and the recent traditions of the Central and Eastern European region.

### III.

The questions raised in chapter II. of the Questionnaire have been mainly formulated because of their logical relation. At the same time we also wished to verify the assumption, that certain classical basic principles do prevail independently of the constitutional position. Beyond the evidence (that the prosecution offices are independent of the courts, these fundamental principles - as a minimum - are as follows: the Prosecution is a centralized, vertically organized institution; its structural units are organised with respect to the court system and the administrative structure of the country; a system of hierarchical subordination and consequently a line of command are prevailing; competences of the subordinated prosecutors may be withdrawn and redistributed by higher prosecutors in individual cases.

As a further fundamental principle may be considered that no other authority or public official can give instructions to the prosecutor, only his own superior; and exception is made when this right is expressly allocated to a defined external agency or person by law. In some of the countries of our region, this special right was allocated to the Minister of Justice, but he is entitled to exercise this right only through the Prosecutor General, - disregarding an abstract situation where the Minister should give instructions through himself, since he himself is the Prosecutor General.

## IV.

The countries of Central and Eastern Europe have tried to adapt the solutions of the elder member states of the Council of Europe in their attempts to transform the "Prokuratura". the establishment of the Bulgarian and Croatian Supreme Council of the Judiciary was evidently inspired by the French "Conseil Supérieur de la Magistrature", just as before the eyes of the Polish legislators could be the image of Anglo-Saxon solutions.

In the course of the adaptation, the elements of the foreign model and of the former national solution were necessarily mixed. An outstanding example of this is the regulation in Romania, where, on the one hand, they adopted the French terminology, so - besides other things - the category of the Prosecutor General's Office, and that of the Prosecutor General by the Supreme Court, while on the other hand, such competences of supervision and control have been given to the above mentioned authority, and dignitary against the territorial prosecution organs, which are not existing in the French model. There, in the French model, the "Procureur général près la Cour de Cassation" has competences exclusively for controlling the work of his own apparatus, that is, regarding his colleagues, working at the Supreme Court, while it is only the Minister of Justice who has competences of supervision and control over the territorial prosecution offices.

In order to emphasize the transformation, some countries have even broken with the name "Prokuratura" traditionally used in Central and Eastern Europe. This is how in the Czech language it has become "Statni zastupitelstvi" (which is the calque of the German- Austrian "Staatsanwaltschaft"), and "Ministerul Public" and "parchet" in Romanian, derivated from French, although the term "Prokuratura" was in both languages, the generally accepted term even before the adaptation of the Soviet model. (In brackets I would like to note that, at the same time, in Poland, where the transformation was taken the furthest, since the operative control of the Prosecution was integrated into the Ministry of Justice, the term "Prokuratura" was not even touched.)

I am deeply convinced that the essence of things is not in their names. In Austria, for example, that is considered as one of the determining models, the prosecution agency by the Supreme Court is still called "Generalprokuratur", while the authority responsible for representing the financial interests of the state is called "Finanzprokuratur". In connection with the names, and also to close my presentation, I would like to share an experience of mine with the participants.

This summer, the top leaders of a French high court and the prosecutor general by this court paid a visit to the leaders of a Hungarian country court and the competent leading prosecutor. One day of the program was organized by the prosecution office, and I was invited.

In my discussions with the French colleagues, I consistently used the terms "Parquet" and "Ministère Public". On the one hand, because these were the terms I considered appropriate on the basis of the French literature, on the other hand, because I did not want to give the impression that I am not for the transformation. The French guests were nodding, but in their phrasing they often used the terms "Procurature", or "Procuratie". In the evening I asked the question: Am I right to use the term "Ministère Public" in general meaning, and the term "Parquet" with regard to individual prosecutional organs, or not? They calmed me by saying that these are the terms indeed that are officially used, but when they want everybody to understand what they mean, they use instead the term "Procurature", or some expression of similar sound.

I do trust that by the end of this conference everybody will understand what we mean, and I hope that this regional report and the subsequent discussion will also contribute to the understanding.

# TOPIC 2

# SELECTION AND STATUS OF PROSECUTORS AND THE MANAGEMENT OF THE PROSECUTOR'S OFFICE

**François CORDIER**
Senior Deputy Prosecutor at the
Paris Regional Court (France)

**Presentation of Topic 2
in its Pan-European context**

Ladies and gentlemen, dear colleagues,

May I first of all express my great pleasure in taking part in this conference and in seeing once more a number of you whom I have already had the honour of meeting, either at Vienna last year or during missions in various countries.

As its title implies, this address will be divided into three parts:

- Recruitment;
- Status;
- Organisation of the Public Prosecutor's Department.

It is quite clear that in the time available I shall be unable to go into too much detail; may I therefore refer you to the written text which I have submitted and which I know I should shorten. I am sure, moreover, that the discussions that we shall be able to have following this address will give you the opportunity to raise any questions that might remain unresolved.

One final preliminary remark: from the aspect of French legislation, I am unable to renew my address in its entirety, since there have been no changes in certain areas since I last spoke to some of you: I therefore ask your forgiveness in advance.

Lastly, it is clear that in my capacity as an officer of the French Public Prosecutor's Department I shall rely on the experiences and legislation of my own country. It is not meant to be a "model" constituting the sole "reference", but the reflection of the efforts of a democratic country, with a republican system, to express in its texts and laws the principles that must govern the Public Prosecutor's Department, which, like the courts, is a guarantor of freedoms. However, the rules elaborated in France are the result of the specificity of our culture, our history and our traditions. The evolution of society and of our institutions, and the ever-increasing influence of international relations and France's place in Europe, have had an effect on the evolution of the Public Prosecutor's Department.

Although I have therefore been led naturally to begin from the French experience, the only one which I have perhaps some legitimacy in addressing, I shall attempt while speaking to you to refer wherever possible to the well-documented answers to the questionnaire of the Council of Europe which you have returned.

\*\*\*\*

**Part 1: Recruitment and training of members of the Public Prosecutor's Department**

**General characteristics**

**Preliminary remark:**

In order to understand the French system fully, it is necessary to realise that in France, as in Belgium or Italy, the Principle of the Unity of the judiciary (*Magistrature*) is applied. This single body includes both judges and prosecutors. This means that in the course of a single career it is possible to serve as judge and prosecutor in turn. It also implies that the rules in the Statutes are to a large extent applicable to both judges and prosecutors, subject to specific rules inherent in the special nature of the duties of the Public Prosecutors Department: prosecutors are responsible for bringing criminal prosecutions and have the specific power to determine whether a prosecution is "appropriate", which they are entitled to do by law (the Code of Criminal Procedure).

Both initial training and continuing training are therefore common to all members of the judiciary, whether they are destined for the bench or the prosecution.

In 1958 the (*École Nationale de la Magistrature*) was established; this was at the initiative of the then Prime Minister, Mr Michel Debré. This establishment was the counterpart of the National School of Administration (*École nationale d'Administration*), which is responsible for the recruitment and training of the Senior Civil Service in France.

The Ecole Nationale de la Magistrature was therefore entrusted with a two-fold mission: first, the initial training of student members of the judiciary (*auditeurs*) and, secondly, the continuing training of all members of the judiciary.

**1. The methods of recruitment of members of the judiciary (prosecutors or judges)**

In France the method of recruitment chosen was to favour the recruitment of judges and public prosecutors from among students of not more than 27 years of age who are university graduates. They must be successful in a national competition and then follow a 31-month course at the Ecole Nationale de la Magistrature.

There is also a second competition for admission to the Ecole Nationale de la Magistrature, which is restricted to public officials of not more than 40 years of age, who need not have a university degree but who must show evidence of four years' service in that capacity. The number of posts in this competition is much more limited.

By way of example, in the first open competition in 1994 110 posts were available, compared with 20 posts in the competition for public officials.

This deliberate choice does not preclude the direct recruitment of judges from among law graduates with several years' experience in the legal field, although this is an additional and much more marginal method; and persons recruited by this method are for the most part required to complete a probationary period in court prior to being integrated.

A. **The recruitment of members of the judiciary via competitions for admission to the Ecole Nationale de la Magistrature**

The choice of competitions as a method of selection is a French tradition that goes back to the Revolution. This procedure makes it possible to guarantee a constitutional principle, namely the principle of equality of opportunity to join, in this case the judiciary, but also more generally the civil service. The practical application of this principle means that all candidates can be assured that selection will be solely on the criteria of their knowledge or abilities, and at the same time that there will be no discrimination based on such considerations as political opinions, membership of a union or religion.

For that purpose, the implementation of competitions assumes the existence of a selection board. This board is appointed by the Minister of Justice, after obtaining the opinion of the Council for the Administration of the Ecole Nationale de la Magistrature, but, once invested with its powers, it is absolutely sovereign in its decisions.

The selection board is sovereign in the appraisal of the scripts, but it is also sovereign in the decision whether or not to fill all the posts offered by the Minister of Justice in a competition. The Minister has no appeal against decisions adopted by the selection board and cannot dispute them. The board's decisions are binding on the Minister: he could not decide, for example, to appoint only some of the candidates accepted (or, should he do so, he would have to recruit all the candidates accepted before opening a new competition).

So that competitions will satisfy their intended purpose in full, two guarantees have been devised:

- **The anonymity of scripts:** the competition for entry to the Ecole Nationale de la Magistrature includes two series of tests: tests to establish eligibility and tests for admission. In order to qualify for the tests for admission a candidate must have been declared eligible, that is he must be among the candidates who have obtained the best results and he must have achieved what the selection board regards as the minimum mark.

(If the selection board considers that the results obtained by the candidates are inadequate, it may very well declare fewer candidates eligible than there are places to be filled.)

The tests for eligibility are purely written tests and are anonymous. This means that, under pain of disqualification, they must not contain any distinguishing sign whereby a candidate might be identified. The administration of the school therefore uses a complex system to ensure that entries are anonymous. Eight accomplices would be necessary before a candidate could find out who would eventually mark his scripts, and even then he would not be absolutely certain. Obviously, all possible steps are taken to ensure that the subjects will remain secret.

- **The guarantees at the level of entry:**

The guarantees provided by the competitions would be illusory if the administration were solely responsible for deciding which candidates could take part in competitions.
The administration is not free in these decisions.

a. The administration is bound by the statutory provisions in force, which are laid down in an organic law. It is the organic law laying down the Statutes of the State Legal Service that determines the conditions which the candidates must meet (conditions regarding age, diploma, morality, health, their position in relation to national service (for students) or length of public service or status for officials).

The majority of these conditions leave no room for interpretation on the part of the administration. Thus if a candidate has exceeded the age limit by one day he cannot be admitted to the competition.

b. Furthermore, a decision refusing to accept an entry must state the reasons on which the administration bases its decision and can form the subject of an appeal before the administrative courts. These courts exercise a very strict control of decisions given in this way, in particular in the area of morality. Thus a decision refusing to admit a candidate to a competition on grounds of morality cannot be based on the candidate's opinions alone, but must be based on the external manifestation of conduct contrary to accepted standards of behaviour or to the discretion which society is entitled to expect of a future member of the judiciary.

Whether they are open to students or to officials, competitions for entry to the Ecole Nationale de la Magistrature consist of the same tests, and the Selection Boards generally choose the same topics.

The tests are intended to ascertain candidates' intellectual qualities, their reasoning abilities and their ability to analyse and draft documents, plus their knowledge of legal matters. The tests cover the whole area of law taught during the four years' study for the master's degree.

Thus the tests for eligibility take the form of four compositions:

- general culture (coefficient 5, length 5 hours);
- civil law (coefficient 4);
- criminal law or public and constitutional law (at the candidate's choice) (coefficient 4);
- summary drafted on the basis of legal documents (coefficient 3).

Admission tests:

- general culture: candidate's choice between a commentary on a text or a general question (coefficient 5);
- the test not chosen in the written test;
- criminal, civil and administrative procedure;
- commercial law or administrative law;
- labour law and social security law;
- test in a living language;
- a sports test (*Mens sana in corpore sano* ...).

I will mention, as a matter of interest, that a third competition has been established, since 1992, by the reform of the organic law. This competition is restricted to persons with eight or more years' professional experience, or who have served one or more terms as a member of an elected assembly of a territorial community, or who have legal experience in a non-professional capacity. These persons do not need to have a law degree and they can take advantage of preparation for the competition organised by the State.

**B.     Direct access to the Ecole Nationale de la Magistrature**

Certain candidates may be accepted to the Ecole Nationale de la Magistrature on the basis of their qualifications. These are persons with a master's degree and four years' experience in the legal, economic or social sphere.

This type of recruitment is also open to doctors of law with two diplomas certifying intensive study and to persons with three years' university teaching experience and a higher degree.

Candidates' files are examined by the Ministry of Justice and submitted to the Promotions Committee, to which both the director of the school and the president of the selection boards for the competitions for entry are appointed. The committee's opinion is binding on the Minister. Candidates recruited in this way are exempt from part of the teaching at the School, instead of which they prepare a thesis. They are also attached to a group recruited by competition.

This form of recruitment is quite insignificant compared with the first two competitions for admission to the Ecole Nationale de la Magistrature.

## C. Direct recruitment to the judicial body

The legislature did not intend to be deprived of this form of recruitment, which should allow the judiciary to attract persons, generally with the degree of master of law, of such a kind as to enrich the corps of judges and prosecutors, who, by virtue of their duties and through the application of the rule of law, are required to have knowledge of many aspects of society.

The following persons may also be appointed to posts in the second grade (the lower grade), provided that they are at least 35 years of age:

- masters of law with seven years' professional experience that particularly qualifies them for legal service;

- senior registrars of courts, tribunals and labour tribunals with seven years' service in that capacity;

- officials in Category A of the Ministry of Justice, provided that they have at least seven years' service in that capacity.

Pursuant to Article 23 of the Statutes of the judiciary, certain persons may be appointed directly to the first grade, first group, of the service, that is to the grade of judge or deputy prosecutor at Courts of Appeal.

These are masters of law with at least 17 years' professional experience that particularly qualifies them for legal service.

Certain senior registrars of the courts and tribunals

Masters of law who fulfil the conditions as regards diploma (Master's degree in law) and have 19 years' professional service that particularly qualifies them for legal service may be appointed to the first grade, second group of the State Legal Service.

It will be noted, as a matter of interest, that university professors of law may in certain conditions, on a proposal from the Judicial Service Commission (Judicial Division), be appointed directly to the Court of Cassation.

The files of candidates for direct recruitment to the judiciary, apart from those referred to in the preceding paragraph, are submitted to the Promotions Committee, which can either reject an application or issue an opinion in favour of the candidate's admission, or first require the candidate to undergo a probationary period which will be organised by the Ecole Nationale de la Magistrature. In this case the candidate will be interviewed by the members of the board responsible for determining the classification of junior members of the judiciary. The results of this probationary period and this interview will eventually be examined by the same committee. The Minister cannot disregard a negative opinion of the committee.

2. **Training at the Ecole Nationale de la Magistrature**

Candidates admitted to the Ecole Nationale de la Magistrature are probationary members of the judicial corps.

In this capacity, they take an oath before the Bordeaux Court of Appeal that they will "scrupulously observe professional secrecy and behave in every way as a worthy and loyal junior member of the judiciary".

Junior members of the judiciary can take part in activities in court under the responsibility of judges or prosecutors, but they do not have any power to take or sign decisions.

They can therefore carry out all the functions of a judge or prosecutor, but under the supervision of the master in charge of their probationary period: they can conduct an inquiry, draft a judgment, take the place of the Public Prosecutor's representative at a hearing, etc.

The Ecole Nationale de la Magistrature, which celebrated its thirtieth anniversary in 1989, has during those years developed a training programme which combines both theory and practice. The school prepares young men and women, the majority of whom are from the universities, for duties in court at the end of 31 months of training.

The programme drawn up by the Ecole Nationale de la Magistrature must "prepare future judges and future members of the Public Prosecutor's Department, not only to exercise their profession in conditions that correspond to the most up-to-date requirements of society, but also to master and adapt themselves to future developments, while retaining the meaning of the specific nature of judicial functions".[1] "Accordingly, the training of members of the judiciary must meet a four-fold requirement: it must prepare junior members to perform the duties associated with the judiciary in their various forms and technical aspects, to ensure that they are in a position to appreciate the social complexity of which judicial activities form part, to know and understand the fundamental principles which underlie and give legitimacy to the intervention of the

---

[1] Introduction to the training programme for junior members of the judiciary, 1992.

judge and, lastly, to acquire a professional culture, which is a necessary condition for a profound understanding of the role and function of the courts."[1]

By way of example, I shall briefly describe the 1992 training programme for junior members of the judiciary.

It included a period of general training spread over 25 months, divided as follows:

- **A long period of training** lasting 13 weeks. These periods of training take place outside the French courts, in a firm, in another administration, with a territorial community or, lastly, abroad. A report must be drawn up.

- **Education actually provided at the School at Bordeaux** (seven and a half months).

This includes:

- introduction to the functions in their entirety, in small groups known as study groups;
- general studies (legal medicine, psychiatry, accounting, etc);
- the discovery of a judicial methodology;
- the study of the general principles of judicial activity, such as the guiding principles of proceedings, the supra-legislative rules: the European Convention for the Protection of Human Rights, but also the statutes of the judiciary;
- study of the judicial environment.

- **A period of 14 months' training in court, where the junior member of the judiciary will carry out all the functions in turn.** This period will be supplemented by short periods with the prison service, the gendarmerie or the police, or in an establishment for the judicial protection of young persons.

**The grading examination**

Although its title gives no indication of this, this examination is extremely important since its purpose is to assess the junior member's suitability to become a member of the judiciary. It is this examination that determines the future of a junior member of the judiciary and his appointment in the corps of members of the judiciary.

The examination consists of a written test and two oral tests:

At the candidate's choice, the drafting of a civil judgment or a prosecutor's written submission, based on actual proceedings (length of test: six hours).

- An oral test on the topic not chosen in the written test, either a prosecutor's oral submissions or civil submissions;

- A conversation with the selection board based on the experience acquired during training;

The total marks awarded in the grading examination are added to the marks for the probationary period and the period of education and give the result and the final grade.

In the light of these tests and the final results obtained, the selection board determines whether a junior member is suitable or unsuitable for the judiciary. The Board may also decide that a junior member who is not sufficiently prepared must do an additional year's studies.

The selection board's decision is sovereign. The board is composed of a judge at the Court of Cassation, an assistant director at the Ministry, a member of the Council of State, two members of the judiciary and two university professors.

Junior members who are declared suitable choose their posts from a list drawn up by the Ministry. The selection board may place restrictions on the duties that can be carried out by certain junior members at the beginning of their career. The junior member's choice may conflict with the unfavourable opinion of the Judicial Service Commission.

Once the grading examination is over, the junior member undergoes a period of education lasting six months. This is both theoretical and practical, but it is confined to the duties which he will carry out in his first appointment.

## Part II: The statutes of the members of the Public Prosecutor's Department

As has already been pointed out, the corps of members of the judiciary includes both judges and members of the Public Prosecutor's Department. The statutes of the judiciary are therefore by definition a single set. They therefore include the provisions common to judges and members of the Public Prosecutor's Department; unlike judges of the bench, however, who are independent and irremovable, members of the Public Prosecutor's Department, because of their special duties, are subject to the authority of the Minister of Justice and are not irremovable.

The guarantees afforded to all members of the judiciary, and therefore enjoyed by members of the Public Prosecutor's Department, have been significantly reinforced in France in recent years, first by an organic law of 25 February 1992 and then by a constitutional amendment in 1993, which was followed by two organic laws of 5 February 1994.

**Section I:** **Provisions common to judges and members of the Public Prosecutor's Department**

**A.** **The rights conferred on members of the Public Prosecutor's Department and judges**

**1.** **Career**

Judges and members of the Public Prosecutor's Department receive the same remuneration, with a few minimal differences as regards the quarterly bonuses associated with their duties.

Their career structure is identical, with the difference that members of the Public Prosecutor's Department number 1,500 compared with 4,500 judges, which necessarily means that there are more senior posts on the bench than in the Public Prosecutor's Department.

In France the career of a member of the judiciary is always characterised by a very strong link between grade and post, in other words a grade corresponds to a particular type of post, which can be exercised only by a judge or prosecutor who has reached that grade.

This principle was made more flexible in 1992, however, by two types of reform:

- An amendment of the organic law, which partly abolished the list of suitability and combined both groups in the second grade (the lower, compared with the first grade). This has the advantage of allowing a more linear development of a career by automatic promotion in steps with a corresponding regular salary increase. This measure favours wider independence by relieving members of the judiciary from over-anxiety about their career, which might have an adverse effect on their independence. This reform was discussed in its principle in spite of its biased character, because there were some who feared that it had the disadvantage of favouring those who were not perhaps the best, to the detriment of the others, and of discouraging the latter.

- The other, according to rather technocratic jargon, was called the "repyramidisation" of posts. This rather obscure language in fact conceals a desire to reclassify certain duties in such a way as to enable careers to progress more favourably, to allow some judges or members of the Public Prosecutor's Department to carry out their duties for longer periods, particularly specialised duties in courts of first instance, or to encourage exchanges between courts of first instance or courts of appeal.

**The career of members of the Public Prosecutor's Department and judges is therefore structured as follows:**

- **Beginning of career:** trainee judge or prosecutor;

- **On appointment as a member of the judiciary:** judge or deputy prosecutor in the **second grade**, investigating judge, children's judge, judge responsible for the execution of sentences, etc.

The <u>minimum</u> period spent in this grade is 10 years.

However, judges or prosecutors with seven years' experience may apply for certain specific posts, such as prosecutor in a small, single-chamber court. They may therefore apply to be entered on a list of suitability for those posts and the promotions committee will decide whether or not they can be entered.

On completion of 10 years' service, although in practice it is generally after a longer period, a deputy prosecutor may be proposed by his superior, the Senior Prosecutor at the regional court, and then by the Senior Prosecutor at the Court of Appeal, for entry on the list for promotion. Apart from the condition relating to length of service, the regulations also require mobility. In order to be entered on the list a candidate must have served in two different courts.

In this case, too, it is the promotions committee that has sovereign power to decide whether or not a candidate is to be entered on the list for promotion.

**Access to the first grade** is conditional upon being entered on that list; the Minister of Justice cannot appoint a candidate who is not on the list to a post in the first grade.

**The first grade is subdivided into two groups:**

- **The first group** (the lower group), which corresponds, in particular, to the post of prosecutor in certain courts with two chambers, or to the post of deputy prosecutor at a Court of Appeal, in other words the post of deputy prosecutor at a court of second instance.

- **The second group** (the higher group), which corresponds, in particular, to the post of prosecutor in certain courts with three chambers, or assistant prosecutor at a provincial Court of Appeal.

Prosecutors in large courts with three chambers may be placed on a special, and therefore higher, salary scale.

Appointments to the second group of the second grade, then to posts outside the standard range, are made by selection by the appointing authority.

**Posts outside the standard range**

These are divided into

- Prosecutors in very large towns and assistant prosecutors at the Paris and Versailles Courts of Appeal.

- Senior prosecutors at the Courts of Appeal.

- Senior Prosecutor at the Paris Court of Appeal, Assistant Prosecutors at the Court of Cassation and Senior Assistant Prosecutor at that court.

- Senior Prosecutor at the Court of Cassation.

**It must be understood that careers in the judiciary, and therefore prosecutors' careers, are highly structured, with a very strong link, albeit less so in recent years, between grade and post. Promotion is essentially on merit and by selection.**

What guarantees are provided to all members of the judiciary as regards the progress of their career?

Two fundamental guarantees must be emphasised here:

<u>First, the existence of the Promotions Committee.</u> It is this committee that decides, in accordance with their merits, on whether judges or prosecutors are to be entered on the list of suitability for certain posts or on the list for promotion. The Minister cannot depart from the committee's opinion.

This committee, whose president is the Senior President of the Court of Cassation, also includes:

- the Senior Prosecutor at the Court of Cassation,;
- two members of the judiciary elected by the court in general assembly;
- two Senior Presidents and two Senior Prosecutors elected by their respective peers;
- ten judges or prosecutors, seven from the second grade and three from the first grade, elected by all members of the judiciary in a ballot in two stages.

As opposed to two heads of division from the Court of Cassation and 16 elected judges, the "administration" is represented only by the Inspector General of Legal Services and the Director of Legal Services.

The committee is therefore for the most part made up of judges and prosecutors elected by their peers; and it has immense powers, since it is entitled to demand information concerning the assessment of a judge or prosecutor who applies to be entered on the list or the promotions table. It can also formulate observations. A judge can appeal to the committee against his "mark".

Furthermore, a judge or prosecutor who has not been proposed by his superiors for entry on the list of suitability or the promotions table can apply directly to the committee.

Lastly, it should be pointed out that a prosecutor is entitled to know where he comes (in comparison with his other colleagues) in the order of names submitted by his superiors.

### The assessment of prosecutors

This assessment must be made every two years by the prosecutor's immediate superior (the Senior Prosecutor at the court), who prepares a draft which is sent to the Senior Prosecutor at the Court of Appeal, who in most cases endorses it.

This assessment is adversarial in so far as it includes a first part drawn up by the prosecutor himself, who has to give an account of his activities and the training that he has received, and is preceded by a interview with his superior.

The assessment is therefore known to the prosecutor, who also has access to his professional file, which must be arranged in such a way that all the documents therein are numbered and initialled, so that no document can be concealed from the person to whom the file relates.

A career in the judiciary, whether as judge or prosecutor, is "for life", that is it generally continues until the statutory age for retirement, except where a judge or prosecutor freely expresses his wish to resign or a disciplinary sanction is ordered by the Judicial Service Commission.

## 2. Protection

Prosecutors are entitled to be protected by their minister against any attack to which they might be subjected, whether physical or mental. Thus a Minister of Justice can take action if a prosecutor has suffered injury or defamation, in order to ensure that prosecutors are protected.

In that regard, it should also be noted - although this time the provisions are in the Criminal Code - that certain offences are aggravated if they are committed against members of the judiciary or the Public Prosecutor's Department (offences involving violence, insults, injury and defamation).

The authorities, and in particular the police or the gendarmerie, are required to ensure freedom of movement for judges and prosecutors in the performance of their duties.

## 3. Other rights

Like judges, members of the Public Prosecutor's Department have the right to form unions. This right has been recognised in the case-law of the Council of State. Membership of a union must not give rise to discrimination and no reference to such membership can be made in the personal file.

There are three magistrates' organisations in France, two of which are professional unions. An association purely for members of the Public Prosecutor's Department has recently been created.

Judges and prosecutors are denied the right to strike, however, since the Statutes prohibit "any concerted action of such a kind as to impede the normal course of justice"

They also have the following rights:

- To benefit from the continuing training provided by the Ecole Nationale de la Magistrature.

- To benefit from the positions and rights of officials that are not contrary to the Statutes of Members of the Judiciary: they may therefore request, and sometimes temporarily obtain, a position on secondment, in order to carry out an activity in another authority or an international organisation, etc.

## B. Obligations common to judges and members of the Public Prosecutor's Department

### 1. Professional secrecy

Before taking up his duties, every member of the judiciary takes an oath that he will "well and faithfully fulfil his duties, scrupulously observe the secrecy of deliberations and behave in every way as a worthy and loyal member of the State Legal Service".

Members of the Public Prosecutor's Department are therefore bound by professional secrecy. They cannot be released from their oath. It will therefore be observed that inquiries carried out by the police or the gendarmerie under the direction of the Public Prosecutor's Department are covered by secrecy. Breach of secrecy is an offence and a disciplinary fault. Judicial inquiries conducted by investigating judges are also covered by secrecy.

It is necessary in our society, however, where events receive a great deal of attention from the media, and where investigative journalism has developed to a very significant degree, that Senior Prosecutors at the regional courts can sometimes provide the media with information designed to avoid any tendentious interpretation of the facts or to prevent false information. This is a very delicate role to carry out, since discretion is mandatory and any prejudice to the presumption of innocence must be avoided.

It must always be remembered, however, that the judicial debate takes place at the stage of the hearing, where all the evidence for the prosecution and the defence is set out and discussed in adversarial proceedings by all the parties, the victim, the accused and the Public Prosecutor's Department. However, it is true that the hearing sometimes comes a long time after the facts and that the case is then no longer of interest to the media, which are much more interested in immediate news, sometimes to the detriment of the presumption of innocence.

## 2. Incompatible functions

### - Electoral office

Article 9 of the order laying down the Statutes contains a list of elected posts the exercise of which, whether by the prosecutor himself or by his spouse, is incompatible with the duties of a member of the Public Prosecutor's Department and, more generally, of a member of the judiciary.

- Membership of the Chamber of Deputies or the Senate, which are national mandates, and also membership of the European Parliament, are entirely incompatible with membership of the judiciary. Any judge or prosecutor elected to one of these assemblies is seconded for the duration of his mandate. Similarly, a judge or prosecutor cannot be a member of the Economic and Social Council.

- Incompatibility is geographically limited to the district covered by the court for the offices of mayor, general or regional councillor or member of other territorial assemblies.

- The spouse of a member of the Chamber of Deputies or the Senate cannot serve as a judge or prosecutor in that member's constituency.

- Incompatibility is temporary and geographically limited in the following cases: a person cannot be a judge or prosecutor in the area in which he held one of the above offices during the previous five years, or in which he unsuccessfully stood for election to such office within the previous three years.

### Professional incompatibilities

A member of the judiciary must devote himself entirely to his office. Accordingly, he cannot hold any other public office or, even more so, any private post (Article 8 of the Statutes).

With the permission of the senior member of his court, however, he may carry out teaching duties or other duties that do not adversely affect his dignity and independence. The possibility for a judge or prosecutor to take part in arbitrations (which are very lucrative) has been restricted by the legislature.

Clearly, a member of the judiciary can undertake literary, artistic or scientific work without permission.

**Family incompatibilities**

These are laid down by the Code of Judicial Organisation and provide that persons related by blood or marriage, or collateral relations, cannot exercise functions together. Certain derogations from this rule may sometimes be envisaged, but it would never be possible, for example, for a husband to act as prosecutor before a chamber presided over by his wife. Relatives can never hear the same case, as their impartiality would be suspect.

3. **The duty of discretion and dignity**

Article 10 of the Statutes expressly requires judges and prosecutors to observe the obligation of discretion: "members of the judiciary shall be prohibited from ... any political demonstration that is incompatible with the discretion which their duties impose on them".

The Statutes of Members of the Judiciary therefore expressly impose on judges and prosecutors an obligation long- since imposed on public officials by the case-law of the Council of State.

It is interesting to note that this obligation of discretion was applied and regarded by the Council of State as being more binding for senior posts, which is also the case for members of the judiciary.

However, it is made more flexible in the context of a mandate in a union.

The obligation applies to candidates for the judiciary, to junior members of the judiciary and serving members of the Public Prosecutor's Department: it also applies to honorary judges.

The obligation of discretion is imposed first of all in the areas set out in Article 43 of the Statutes, on discipline:

*"honour, delicacy and dignity" in private life.*

Any deliberate criminal offence clearly constitutes a breach of this obligation (examples referred to the disciplinary committee include theft, living on immoral earnings by cohabiting with a prostitute, breach of the secrecy of the investigation, accepting bribes or being involved in corrupt practices)

The following may also be regarded as being in breach of the obligation, however: drunkenness, a way of life that is too hectic and contrary to the image that the public are entitled to expect of a member of the judiciary, excessive indebtedness and being pursued by creditors, intimate relations with litigants susceptible of causing dysfunctions and faults in the administration of the proceedings.

Other breaches of that obligation consist in "failure to uphold the duties of his status" in the context of professional life. This means misuse of office, abuse of office or the complete failure to do any work.

In return for the salary which he is paid, a member of the judiciary is under what is called an obligation "for service provided".

It will be observed that work in court, and especially the content of decisions, cannot be attacked from the disciplinary angle, in particular as regards judges of the bench, since to do so would be contrary to their independence. **A judicial decision can be called in question only by means of an appeal.** Criticism in a newspaper or during an interview of a decision delivered by a colleague is unquestionably a fault.

**The obligation of reserve expressly extends to a judge's political life.**

Although a judge or prosecutor, like every citizen, is free to have political opinions, or even to belong to a political party, it is stipulated that members of the judiciary are prohibited from any deliberation of a political nature and from "displaying any hostility towards the principle or the form of the Government of the Republic".

These provisions are not prejudicial to their political rights in their capacity as citizens but they do reduce the extent to which those rights can be displayed or demonstrated in public. The specific role of the judge and prosecutor in civic life actually makes it preferable - according to the formula of Mr. Darcos, a former Deputy Director of the Judicial Department at the Ministry - that their political opinions should not be openly exhibited. Their personal choices must remain confined to the spheres of their civic life and not be paraded in their social role so that they will not be suspected of bias, or even of failing to observe the principle of the separation of powers.

"Although the discretion imposed by law on members of the corps of judges and prosecutors does not call in question their freedom of expression, it none the less prevents them from adopting any position that might give rise to doubt as regards their neutrality" (Darcos, cited above).

Therefore, while members of the judiciary, and in particular their unions, may express their opinions on, and possibly criticise, a law that is in the process of being drafted, they must silence these criticisms once the law has been passed, since they are responsible for applying the law and the law represents the expression of the will of the nation.

4. **Other obligations**

**The obligation of residence**

Judges and prosecutors are required to reside in the area covered by the court in which they serve. A derogation may be granted to them by the Minister, however, on a favourable proposal from the senior member of the court.

**The obligation to undergo training**

This obligation follows directly from the Statutes and from the duties associated with the status of a member of the judiciary. Judges and prosecutors must ensure that their knowledge is kept up to date. Despite the positive efforts of the Ministry of Justice, including the right to training by means of continuing training sessions organised by the Ecole Nationale de la Magistrature, the distribution of documents by the Ministry, etc., it must none the less be accepted that the workload of both prosecutors and judges means that they must sacrifice their free time to take advantage of this training.

## Section II: Provisions specific to members of the Public Prosecutor's Department

**Unlike judges, members of the Public Prosecutor's Department in France are not irremovable: furthermore, they are subject to the authority of their superiors**

**A.    The command structure**

Pursuant to Article 5 of the law on the statutes of the judiciary, "members of the Public Prosecutor's Department shall be placed under the direction and control of their superiors and under the authority of the Minister of Justice".

This principle, which is developed in the Code of Judicial Organisation as regards the organisation of the members of the Public Prosecutor's Department, is explained and expressed in a number of provisions of the Code of Criminal Procedure.

Thus Article 33 of the Code provides that the prosecutor is to make written submissions to the court in accordance with the instructions of the Senior Prosecutor.

Article 36 of the Code of Criminal Procedure provides that the Minister of Justice may report any criminal offences of which he is aware to the Senior Prosecutor and order him, by instructions in writing which are added to the case file, to commence proceedings or have proceedings commenced or to lodge with the competent court such written submissions as the Minister may deem appropriate.

Under Article 37, the Senior Prosecutor at each Court of Appeal has authority over all the members of the Public Prosecutor's Department in the district covered by the Court of Appeal.

Similarly, Article 44 of the Code gives the Senior Prosecutor at each regional court authority over the members of the Public Prosecutor's Department in the District Courts within his area.

- **The basis of the principle:**

In France the basis of the principle of the command structure of the Public Prosecutor's Department derives from two closely-linked sources:

The principle of legitimacy: unlike the government in a democratic State such as France, prosecutors do not rely for their legitimacy on universal suffrage. Their legitimacy derives from the fact that they are appointed by the President of the Republic on a proposal from the Minister of Justice.

The government are accountable, through periodic elections, to the electorate, that is to all citizens. A government may therefore have to account for the functioning of the criminal justice system and in particular for the conduct of prosecutions. If the government are accountable for the criminal justice system they must have the means of controlling its actions.

Furthermore - and this question cannot be dissociated from the previous question - it should be noted that in France the power to determine whether it is appropriate to bring proceedings has been conferred on the Public Prosecutor's Department.

Although under Article 31 of the Code of Criminal Procedure the Public Prosecutor's Department is to bring prosecutions and demand the application of the law, Article 40 provides that the Senior Prosecutor at the regional court is to receive complaints **and determine what measures are to be taken in relation thereto.**

Because of this discretionary - and that does not mean arbitrary - power, the need to standardise the practices of the various prosecutors, while respecting the diversity of local contexts, and to ensure that all citizens are equal before the criminal law, makes necessary the Authority of the Minister of Justice, the Minister of a Government which are accountable to parliament and also to the electorate at the time of elections.

**The scope of the power of the command structure**

**What instructions can be given to the prosecutors?**

**Instructions of a general nature**

The government, who are accountable to the electorate for their actions, implement a criminal policy. They also intend that the criminal laws that are voted, or that the government have adopted by parliament because they think them appropriate, should be applied. The government assess the effectiveness of their criminal policy on the basis of the reports which are submitted to them.

It is therefore accepted in France that the Minister of Justice is authorised to issue general directives, which may be of various types:

Some of these will be extremely useful commentaries on laws which have just been approved. Thus when the new Criminal Code was published an explanatory circular of more than three hundred pages was distributed. Likewise, the Ministry of Justice sent its services and published answers to the legal questions which arose. Of course, these explanations are valid only as long as they are not contradicted by judicial decisions.

Some circulars express the Minister's desire to remind members of the prosecution of the interest in pursuing a particular offence, or of favouring a particular prosecution method because it is quicker or more effective.

All these various circulars are designed to encourage a unified practice throughout the national territory.

The issue which has been the subject of most discussion in France has always concerned instructions relating to particular cases, and there has sometimes been great temptation to see in the power to issue such instructions a power that was susceptible of preventing certain cases from succeeding.

It is essential to put that question clearly and dispassionately in perspective:

- Since they act under the authority of the Minister of Justice, it is normal that Senior Prosecutors at the Regional Courts should keep the Minister informed of particularly serious cases or of those of particular public interest in their area.

- The number of cases indicated in this way is trivial compared with the number of new cases, which rose to 5,431,477 in 1992.

- The majority of reports will therefore contain only information or a statement and will not call for any response, still less for approval.

It is none the less appropriate that cases should be indicated in accordance with their gravity, as I have already observed, and not according to the identity or function of the persons involved, which might cause the Senior Prosecutor at the Regional Court to relinquish his own authority.

The second reason for these indications or reports is that the Senior Prosecutor at the Regional Court wishes to contact his superior about the most appropriate way of concluding a criminal case, which is not always as evident as it might appear. In that case the communication is sent to the Senior Prosecutor at the Court of Appeal, who, where he approves of it, forwards it to the Ministry. It is then dealt with by the Department of Criminal Matters and Pardons.

There may be a third explanation for these reports, where there is a request for the Ministry's agreement on the solutions to be applied in a particular case.

These reports raise the delicate question - in addition to the answers above - of the extent to which the Ministry is authorised to intervene in criminal proceedings. Might a Government not be tempted to slow certain proceedings down, to speed others up, etc., for reasons that have nothing to do with those of justice, a situation that by its very nature can only be disturbing?

This question has been very widely debated in France during recent years, to such a point that the present Minister of Justice has established non-intervention in criminal matters as a principle of action.

As I have already observed, it is necessary to put the question in its proper perspective and not to exaggerate its scope.

The problem, although it concerns serious criminal cases, is none the less limited to a very small number of proceedings. Above all, however, its extension is prevented by three other factors of a different order:

- Members of the Public Prosecutor's Department are highly conscious, first, of the fact that they are members of the judiciary and, secondly, of their duties and responsibilities. Nor should the fact that they may also wish to become judges one day be underestimated.

- The freedom of the press in a democracy. In a true democracy, and especially where investigative journalism is developed, it is difficult, indeed impossible, to maintain secrecy in a criminal case. This power of the press is considerable and it has a definite influence.

- **BUT, ABOVE ALL, THE LAW**

The law has placed limits on the power of the Minister of Justice to intervene in prosecutions.

Thus the Minster of Justice or the Senior Prosecutors at the Courts of Appeal can only order prosecutions to be brought; they cannot forbid them.

The power to initiate the prosecution belongs solely to Senior Prosecutors at the Regional Courts, and no-one can take their place.

The Minister's instructions must be in writing and must be attached to the file relating to the proceedings, which constitutes a serious guarantee. This very appropriate reform was introduced very recently.

The victim of an offence can still commence proceedings on his own initiative, either by bringing a private prosecution or by lodging a complaint before an investigating judge, together with a claim for civil damages. No-one can prevent these proceedings from continuing unless there are statutory grounds for doing so.

French law, and in particular the Statutes and the Code of Criminal Procedure, lay down the maxim "The pen is in serfdom, the word is free" (Arts 5 and 33 respectively). This maxim underlines the independence of prosecutors, because they belong to the corps of members of the judiciary.

This fundamental principle was emphasised in a decision of the Prosecutors' Disciplinary Committee delivered on 9 October 1987:

> "... freedom of speech at the hearing, which is expressly provided for in Article 5 of the Statutes, has the effect of removing the prosecutor from the authority and control of his superiors, and also from the authority of the Minister of Justice, so that he is subject only to the dictates of his own conscience ... the Order [laying down the Statutes] enshrines the principle of the unity of members of the judiciary ... the independence of members of the Public Prosecutor's Department is the same as that of judges, save as regards certain provisions concerning irremovability and the competence of the Judicial Service Commission[2], ... the particular rules to which members of the Public Prosecutor's Department are subject are based solely on the nature of their duties, since the exercise of prosecutions explains and justifies the powers conferred by law on the Minister of Justice;

> "... claiming that members of the Public Prosecutor's Department were entirely subject to a command structure with the Minister of Justice at its head would, as has often been observed, only discredit justice by making prosecutors simply representatives of the executive power.

> "The Public Prosecutor's Department serves the law; it is from the law alone that it derives its mission, and it is to the law alone that its members must account for mistakes which they make in court".

- It should finally be added that the fact that during their career members of the Public Prosecutor's Department may become judges is of such a kind as to ensure that they perform their duties properly.

---

[2] This decision was delivered before the establishment of the division of the Judicial Service Commission that is competent for members of the Public Prosecutor's Department.

This last remark leads me to consider the career guarantees henceforward given to prosecutors (in the wide sense).

## Guarantees specific to the career of members of the Public Prosecutor's Department

### Guarantees in relation to appointments

It will be recalled that guarantees are given in relation to a prosecutor's career. I have already mentioned the Promotions Committee, composed for the most part of elected judges and prosecutors, which has sovereign power to appraise the qualities of judges and prosecutors applying for promotion. I must now point out the additional guarantees given to prosecutors following the constitutional reform of 1993.

Until that date, if we ignore the short period between 1992 and 1993 when an Advisory Committee of the Public Prosecutor's Department had been established, the appointment of members of the Public Prosecutor's Department depended solely on the President of the Republic, who acted on a proposal from the Minister of Justice.

Henceforth appointments to the prosecution, except to the posts of Senior Prosecutors at the Courts of Appeal and prosecutors at the Court of Cassation, are submitted for the opinion of the Prosecution Division of the Judicial Service Commission.

Until 1993 the Judicial Service Commission, a body established by the Constitution (Articles 64 and 65 of the Constitution) was competent only in relation to judges. It now includes a division which is competent for members of the Public Prosecutor's Department. Admittedly, the powers of this division are not as great as those of the division responsible for judges, but it represents definite progress.

The division of the Commission responsible for members of the prosecution is therefore charged with stating its opinion on virtually all proposals for appointments prepared by the Minister of Justice.

The Commission gives a simple opinion, which is not binding on the Minister. At present it is too early to say whether the Minister will follow the opinions of the Commission and therefore those unfavourable to the Minister. It will be noted that previously where the opinion given by the Commission in relation to judges was "simple" (advisory) and inconsistent with the Minister's views, as at present, the President of the Republic had never departed from the opinion. In my view, however, the question might be viewed differently where members of the prosecution are concerned.

- **The composition of the Prosecution Division of the Judicial Service Commission**

The Prosecution Division of the Judicial Service Commission includes:

- President: the President of the Republic;
- Vice-President: the Minister of Justice;
- a member of the judiciary from outside the standard range of posts, an assistant prosecutor at the Court of Cassation elected by the assistant prosecutors in general assembly;
- a senior prosecutor elected by all the senior prosecutors;
- a prosecutor elected by all the prosecutors;
- two members of the prosecution and one judge elected according to a system of election in two rounds;
- a Councillor of State, common to both divisions of the Commission, elected by the Council of State in general assembly;

- three individuals, common to both divisions, appointed by the President of the Republic, the President of the Senate and the President of the National Assembly, respectively.

**Observations:**

1. The representativeness of the Commission is therefore ensured in two ways: first by the presence of persons from outside, who increase the legitimacy of the Commission by the presence of persons of unquestionable standing nominated by the three highest authorities of the State (the individuals nominated, who cannot belong to the world of politics, are at present an ambassador of France, a professor of law and a former president of the order of advocates).

2. Members of the judiciary, who are in the majority in the division. The question has been discussed whether, to avoid any risk of corporatism, it might have been preferable to have had a better balance between persons from outside and members of the judiciary.

As may be observed, voting is by a majority, but the purpose of the inclusion of the first three categories is to satisfy the desire to see three representatives of the highest authority sitting in the Prosecution Division of the Commission, in view of the tasks assigned to it.

The ballot for the election of the three other members of the judiciary, representing the two first grades, is in two stages. All the voters of the prosecution first elect, by a uninominal vote in one stage, 80 "grand electors", who must have five years' actual service and be in office. The latter elect the two representatives to the Prosecution Division of the Commission, while the 160 judge-electors elect their representative to the Prosecution Division of the Commission.

### Rules applicable to members of the Judicial Service Commission

**The length of the mandate is four years, and it cannot be renewed immediately.**

During this period members of the Judicial Service Commission cannot receive any advancement or promotion, nor can they receive any decoration.

They may be either seconded or released from their duties so that they can carry out their duties in full; the latter solution is generally chosen.

They receive compensation and are bound by professional secrecy.

The Commission is assisted by an administrative secretary, who may himself be assisted by a deputy, both of whom are appointed by Decree of the President of the Republic, countersigned by the Minister of Justice and the Prime Minister.

### Functions and attributions

As a general rule the Judicial Service Commission, whether the Prosecution Division or the Judicial Division, functions as a restricted committee, that is without the presence of the President of the Republic or the Minister of Justice and under the presidency of a president chosen by the body itself.

The Prosecution Division considers proposals for appointment which have been drawn up for the Public Prosecutor's Department by the Ministry and which have been distributed to all members of the Judiciary.

For the purpose of considering those proposals, the division appoints a rapporteur, who has access to:

- the list of candidates for the posts to be filled, together with their length of service in the judiciary and grade (applications for posts in the same grade or for promotion);

- candidates' files, including the file of the candidate chosen by the Ministry;

- the Council may decide to interview candidates or to obtain any supplementary information which it deems appropriate.

The Council therefore does not carry out a single, intrinsic examination of applications, but subjects them to an extrinsic examination, which constitutes an undeniable guarantee.

This preparatory work was previously carried out (although at that time solely in relation to judges) by a meeting with the Director of Judicial Services (at the Ministry). At the end of the discussion the Commission would inform the Director of the opinion which would be stated in the presence of the Minister. It was customary for the Minister to withdraw his proposal if it was not approved. At present it is too early, in the light of the difference in nature between the duties of the bench and those of the prosecution, and of the recent establishment of the Prosecution Division of the Commission, to know whether that practice will endure.

**Note: It is absolutely necessary to emphasise at this juncture that the extrinsic examination of applicants' documents by the Prosecution Division of the Commission** is also made possible by **the right of complaint recognised to any candidate who is rejected. The candidate may lodge a complaint with the Commission. In this document he will be careful not to criticise the candidate chosen by the Ministry, but he will be able to put forward the arguments based on length of service, grade and professionalism which he believes may operate in his favour.**

Since only the names of candidates selected for the posts to be filled are published, unsuccessful candidates know where they stand only in relation to the successful candidates. Previously the names of all candidates were published, and the one selected was indicated. It is to be feared that this change, apart from not being favourable to transparency, will encourage an increase in appeals and will unnecessarily increase the work of the Commission.

**Second point to be emphasised: The Prosecution Division of the Commission has no power to make proposals: it can either accept the Ministry's suggestion or reject it. If that negative opinion is followed the mechanism for appointment must be commenced again from the beginning.**

It may therefore be concluded that the guarantees in relation to appointments have been greatly increased in recent years and that this additional protection will inevitably facilitate an impartial exercise of the prosecution, since it must never be forgotten that the guarantees given to prosecutors or judges are provided in the interest of those subject to the law.

**Whatever the legislative system chosen, it is essential that the members of the Public Prosecutor's Department have sufficient autonomy to carry out their duties.**

I cannot complete this address without briefly mentioning the disciplinary system applicable to prosecutors.

As I have already pointed out, "any failure to observe honour, scrupulousness and dignity in his private life and any failure in the duties associated with his status" constitute faults susceptible of being punished with a disciplinary sanction.

In the light of the responsibilities given to prosecutors, it is essential that the disciplinary rules applicable to them should be rigorously enforced. That constitutes an undeniable guarantee.

First of all, you must be aware that prosecutors do not enjoy any special immunity - apart from the immunity arising from freedom of speech at the hearing, which is not completely unrestricted - and that they do not enjoy any privilege as regards the courts before which they are accountable.

In the event of a breach of the criminal law, they can be prosecuted before the ordinary courts like every citizen. In the event of a breach of discipline, prosecutors can be the subject of disciplinary proceedings upon application by the Ministry of Justice.

These proceedings will be conducted by the inspectorate of the judicial services. In the most serious cases prosecutors can be suspended, but in this case the proceedings must be very quickly transferred to the Judicial Service Commission, failing which the suspension will be void.

The disciplinary authority is then the Prosecution Division of the Commission, but under the presidency of the Senior Prosecutor at the Court of Cassation.

The hearing is in camera and adversarial. The Director of Judicial Services supports the indictment and the prosecutor charged can be assisted by one or more counsel.

Sanctions range from a reprimand in the prosecutor's file to compulsory transfer, withdrawal from certain duties, being moved to a lower scale, being downgraded, compulsory retirement and dismissal.

### Part III: The organisation of the Public Prosecutor's Department

The Public Prosecutor's Department is not organised as an administrative entity. The Public Prosecutor's Department has its own internal command structure and its secretariat-registry, **but it forms an integral part** of each court of the judicial order.

Thus the Regional Courts (courts of first instance), the Courts of Appeal (courts of second instance) and the Court of Cassation consist of judges, members of the Public Prosecutor's Department and the registry (officials).

The President and the Senior Prosecutor of the court administer it together. They therefore allocate the officials and decide on the budgetary expenses, with the assistance of the Senior Registrar. Clearly, each remains master in his own domain. Thus the Senior Prosecutor cannot interfere with the allocation of judges, which would be prejudicial to their independence. Similarly, the President cannot meddle in the internal organisation of the prosecution.

The organisation of the prosecution is structured. The Senior Prosecutor is surrounded, according to the size of the court, by assistant prosecutors, senior deputy prosecutors, deputy prosecutors, etc, in greater or fewer numbers.

It will be recalled, however, that members of the Public Prosecutor's Department derive their power directly from the law and that they do not act by delegation from their superiors. None the less, they are subordinated to the Senior Prosecutor and are under a duty of loyalty to him. The principle of indivisibility implies that each member of the prosecution is supposed to speak on behalf of all its members.

The organisation of the prosecution is also structured as follows:

- Ministry of Justice;
- Senior Prosecutors at the Courts of Appeal;
- Prosecutors at the Regional Courts;
- Prosecutors at the District Courts.

**Observations:**

The Senior Prosecutor at the Court of Cassation carries out his duties only at that court; he has no authority over the Senior Prosecutors at the Courts of Appeal, of whom there are 35.

The Ministry of Justice provides the intellectual and material resources of the courts. The action of the Ministry is implemented by its directorates:

| | |
|---|---|
| Legal directorates: | Directorate of Civil Matters |
| | Directorate of Criminal Matters and Pardons |
| | Services of European and International Matters |
| Operating directorates: | Directorate of Judicial Services |
| | Directorate of General Matters |
| | Prisons Directorate |

Because of their duties, prosecutors are most often in contact with the Directorate of Criminal Matters and Pardons.

That brings me to the end of this presentation of the Public Prosecutor's Department, and of recruitment, training, its statutes and its organisation. As our society has changed, this very old French institution has seen its functions continue to increase and diversify. As a representative of society, the Public Prosecutor's Department has been able to adapt to developments and remain the guarantor of freedoms that it is required to be, whether in the exercise of the prosecution or in its role in the civil or commercial courts.

It is in its day-to-day activities, which are often obscure and ignored, that it must defend our fellow citizens by applying the criminal law, while always taking care to respect the great principles which must inspire its activities, the principles of the Declaration of Human Rights and those of the European Convention on Human Rights.

## TOPIC 2

## SELECTION AND STATUS OF PROSECUTORS AND THE MANAGEMENT OF THE PROSECUTOR'S OFFICE

**Ilona LÉVAI**
**Head of Division**
**Prosecutor General's Office (Hungary)**

### General Presentation of the solutions of Central and Eastern European countries

This report has been concluded by 25 September 1994, and is based on national reports from 10 countries: Albania, Belarus, Bulgaria, Croatia, the Former Yugoslav Republic of Macedonia, Poland, Romania, the Russian Federation, the Slovak Republic and Slovenia. From 6 countries reports have not been received prior to the deadline set for their presentation (15 September 1994). Assuming the task of preparing the questionnaire as well as the honor of giving regional rapporteurs, Hungary has not prepared a national report. All regional rapporteurs deal with the specific Hungarian solutions in their synthesis report.

I am grateful to those who have sent the co-organizers a national report in time. These reports have helped me considerably in drafting this report. I appreciate the efforts of those who have prepared them, especially because all preparatory work connected to this meeting was primarily Mr. Hlavathy's and my own responsibility. So, let me express our gratitude for your co-operation.

At the same time I would like to apologize for not being able to give you an overall picture on the endeavours made in the Central and East European region to transform the prosecutorial organisation. The lack of information explains why regional reports are somewhat unbalanced, and indeed incomplete, by referring exclusively only 11 countries.

Before summarizing the answers given to the individual points of the questionnaire, some introductory remarks seem to be appropriate:

First, the status of prosecutors could have far-reaching implications for the requirements of fairness and impartiality that the prosecutorial activities should meet in a State governed by law. The Public Prosecution Office as a state organ may have different positions in the constitutional structure. Its actual position may highly influence, at least in principle, the decision-making process of individual prosecutors in specific cases. On the other hand, it could hardly be denied that the status of prosecutors which embraces their rights and obligations, the selection process, the promotion and disciplinary system could also be decisive not only to the individual decision-making process, but to the functioning of the prosecutorial organ as a whole. As a result, we have to distinguish between the position of the institution and the position of individual prosecutors.

Second, in most countries of the former Eastern bloc prosecutors and judges were not the beloved ones of the old regimes; they were "workers" under the terms of the Labour Code. They did not enjoy any privileges, self-governmental rights or rights to representation of professional interests. Thus, the sophisticated regulation of the status of prosecutors and judges which is one of the characteristics of many Western systems is unknown in the Eastern region of Europe. The countries of the region made a lot of progress in this field, but there is still a long way to go.

Third, in the Continental Europe it can be regarded as a tradition dating back to the early 19th century that prosecutors are appointed and not elected. Since Napoleon I established the modern prosecutorial organization, prosecutors have, at least in the Western part of Europe, always been appointed by the Head of State. We must not forget, however, that in certain countries of the Eastern part of Europe during the communist era prosecutor generals and even other prosecutors were elected by parliament. It cannot be denied that the "election" was a formal one, and it should be considered an appointment.

III.1. The 11 countries whose prosecutorial system is now analyzed can be divided into three groups. <u>The first group</u> is of those that maintained the independent constitutional position of the Public Prosecution Office in its form inherited from the old regime (Belarus, Former Yugoslav Republic of Macedonia, Slovak Republic, Russia, Slovenia and Hungary). In these countries the Public Prosecution Office is independent from the executive and connected only to the parliament. <u>The second group</u> consists of those countries which created a new type of independence (Albania, Bulgaria, Croatia). In these countries the Public Prosecution Office became part of the judiciary. <u>The third group</u> comprises two countries (Poland and Rumania) where the Office is subordinated to the executive, i.e. to the Minister of Justice.

<u>In the first group</u> the pattern of election is followed only in two countries (Belarus and Hungary). In Hungary, the Prosecutor General is elected by Parliament at the proposal of the President of the Republic for a term of 6 years. His term is separated from the 4 year term of the legislative. All the other prosecutors are appointed by him, except his deputies who are appointed at his proposal by the President of the Republic for an indefinite time.

In all the other countries having prosecutorial organization with an old type of independence, the prosecutor general is appointed. In the Russian Federation the Prosecutor General is appointed by the Federal Council of the Russian Federation's Assembly at the proposal of the President of Russia. Other prosecutors are appointed by him, but before appointing a prosecutor to a Member State of the Russian

Federation, he is obliged to consult with the State concerned. In turn, the Prosecutor General in the Slovak Republic is appointed by the President of the Republic at the proposal of the highest legislative body. Other prosecutors are appointed by him.

Slovenia and Macedonia have an unique solution in this group. In these countries all prosecutors, including the Prosecutor General, are appointed by the highest legislative body: in the Former Yugoslav Republic of Macedonia at the proposal of the Government, in Slovenia at the proposal of the Prosecutor General (we do not know at whom proposal the latter is appointed). In Macedonia, all prosecutors are responsible not only to their superiors, but to Parliament as well. It would be interesting to see how this construction of double responsibility operates in practice and in what way ordinary prosecutors are accountable to the highest legislative body. To my knowledge, prosecutors of these two countries were elected by assemblies of federation even during the era when they were part of Yugoslavia.

The second group of countries where the Public Prosecution Office is independent by being part of the judiciary have created a new organ: a High Judiciary Council. The inspiration was probably taken from France, Portugal or Italy. Unfortunately, we have little information about the composition of this new and very important body which is probably the highest administrative organ of the judiciary. Only the national report received from Croatia gives details, saying that the High Judiciary Council has 14 members and a president. They are elected by the House of Representatives of the Parliament for a term of 8 years and the candidates are eminent judges, prosecutors, defence lawyers and professors of law. As the High Judiciary Council in many respects has taken over the functions exercised earlier by the Head of State, the Parliament or the Minister of Justice, it would be useful to know by what constitutional techniques political neutrality or political well balancing of this body is assured and how it operates in the everyday practice (whether it has an administrative staff, how decisions are prepared, etc.).

In Croatia all prosecutors, including the Prosecutor General, are appointed by the High Judiciary Council. The term of office of the Prosecutor General and other high ranking prosecutors is 8 years. The other prosecutors are appointed for life. This continuity of service is regarded as a guarantee of the independence in work. In Bulgaria prosecutors are also appointed by the High Judiciary Council, with one exception. The Prosecutor General is appointed by the President of the Republic and the Council is empowered only to nominate candidates for the post of the Prosecutor General. Nevertheless, the President of the Republic is not allowed to refuse appointment after a second nomination of the same person, which underlines that the Council is able to enforce its will against the head of state. The most surprising solution is that of Albania. Even though the prosecution organ is part of the judiciary, the appointment of the Prosecutor General and his deputies follows the pattern of election referred to in the first group: they are elected by parliament. Other prosecutors are appointed but we do not know by whom. As to the proceedings of nomination to be followed before a decision, we have not received answer.

Though Rumania belongs to the third group, it has a High Judiciary Council, too. We do not know of whom it is composed. We only think that its composition follows the French model, and it is presided by the President of the Republic and the Minister of Justice is one of its members. Otherwise, prosecutors, including the Prosecutor General, are elected by the President of the Republic at the proposal of the High Judiciary Council.

In Poland, the Minister of Justice is the Prosecutor General. So, he is appointed and removed in his capacity of member of the Government. The Deputy Prosecutor General, who actually directs the prosecutorial activities, is appointed and removed from his post by the Prime Minister at the request of the Minister of Justice. Other prosecutors are appointed by the Minister of Justice.

III.2. In all countries from which we have received answers, prosecutors have to have a degree in law. No postgradual studies are required, but a successful professional exam prescribed for prosecutors after a certain period of apprenticeship is generally necessary. In some countries there is an age limit: prosecutors in Slovakia should be at least 24 years old, in Poland 26 years, and according to the draft law of Slovenia 30 years.

III.3. With the exception of the Russian Federation and Slovenia, party membership and political activities are expressly prohibited for prosecutors. In Russia, within the prosecutorial organization only the establishment and functioning of political parties or their local organizations is expressly prohibited. In Slovenia, the functions performed in bodies of political parties are incompatible with the function of prosecutor.

All this certainly is a reaction to the requirements of the past when party membership was generally necessary to become a prosecutor or to be promoted. It may well be that in the West prosecutors are free to affiliate themselves with political parties and they have only the obligation to remain reserved about their political conviction which is part of their privacy. It is also true that the UN Guidelines on the Role of Prosecutors state: "Prosecutors, like other citizens are entitled to freedom of expression, belief, association and assembly". Even if so, it is questionable whether the restrictions imposed on prosecutors (and judges) in the new or restored democracies should be lifted. In the draft law on rules of service of the Hungarian prosecutors there are optional provisions in this respect. One of them would be to lift the political restriction for certain categories of legal staff of the Public Prosecutor's Office, namely for apprentices, legal secretaries and investigators. Even though these people are not prosecutors, I do not think this option would be a healthy solution in a country where public services were overpoliticised for several decades and the everyday political culture an behaviour is somehow differs from that of the traditional democracies.

In most countries only activities of an academic, artistic or pedagogic character are compatible with the profession of prosecutors. In some countries activities of economic nature are expressly prohibited, and public functions, with certain exceptions, are also qualified as incompatible with the prosecutorial function.

III.4. The rules of promotion are, as the experience of many Western countries shows, of crucial importance among the guarantees of moral integrity of individual prosecutors and high moral standard required from prosecutors in their capacity of guardian of law. That is the reason why many Western countries have built into their promotion system some automatic elements and try to define precisely the criteria for the evaluation of prosecutors. In other words, the promotion system should be transparent and the carrier of prosecutors should be calculable.

If we look at the four countries which have a High Judiciary Council, we find different solutions. Albania has no special rules on promotion and prosecutors are evaluated in a practical way. The national report acknowledges that the promotion system is not transparent. We have no information whether the High Judiciary Council has any competence in the promotion process. In Bulgaria, prosecutors are promoted at the proposal of the Prosecutor General by the High Judiciary Council. There is no systematic promotion system, generally the interest of the office determines the assessment of the Prosecutor General. Croatia has an evaluation system with well defined criteria. Unfortunately, we do not know whether the High Judiciary Council or other organ is competent in promotion cases. In Rumania, the Minister of Justice decides on promotion cases at the proposal of the Prosecutor General. Prosecutors can only be promoted or transferred with their consent. We have only general information on the criteria of promotion (some years in service, valuable activity). The value of the activity is attested by the superior prosecutors and the prosecutor inspectors.

In addition to Albania, Bulgaria and Rumania, there is no systematic evaluation and promotion system in Hungary, Macedonia, Poland, Slovakia and currently in Slovenia. In Belarus and the Russian Federation there are special rules of promotion and special commissions for evaluating prosecutors. In Russia, the promotion of prosecutors is planned and the evaluation is effectuated publicly.

In Slovenia where prosecutors are appointed for a term of 8 years, the draft law envisages an unlimited term of office and the right to be promoted. The draft law also would bring prosecutors on an equal position with judges and contains an elaborated promotion system with well defined criteria.

After this overview we have the impression that only Belarus and the Russian Federation have preserved their promotion system. The bulk of the other countries seems to be in a real transitional period where the old system has already abandoned and a new one has not established yet.

III.5. It is only one aspect of the legal status of prosecutors, who are generally obliged to follow the instructions of their superiors, that it would be dangerous if they may be dismissed any time upon demonstration of a greater commitment towards the principles of the administration of justice than to the policies of the government. The legal conditions of disciplinary actions taken against prosecutors, the question of the disciplinary authorities as well as the judicial remedies the prosecutors may use against the disciplinary decision are of high importance.

Of the 4 countries that have a High Council of Judiciary, only in 3 countries (Albania, Bulgaria and Croatia) does this organ have competence in disciplinary matters. In Rumania, disciplinary proceedings are initiated by the Minister of Justice or the Prosecutor General. The preliminary investigation is conducted by the inspector prosecutor and its result is submitted to the Board of Discipline of the Public Prosecution Office (the latter in the English text is mentioned as "Public Ministry", but we think this is the word for word translation of the French "ministère public"). The Board decides the case. The decision of the Board can be attacked before the Supreme Court. The law strictly defines the conditions of the removal of prosecutors from their office.

From the national report sent by Albania, the competence of the High Council of Judiciary is not totally clear to us. In Bulgaria, disciplinary rules and proceedings currently is governed by the Labour Code and no judicial control is provided. If the recently passed Judiciary Branch Act enters into force, the most serious disciplinary sanctions may only be imposed by the High Judiciary Council at the proposal of the Prosecutor General. The decision may be appealed before the Supreme Court. In Croatia, where the disciplinary offenses are, according to the national report, strictly defined, the High Judiciary Council deals with each disciplinary case.

In the Former Yugoslav Republic of Macedonia the disciplinary authority is the Disciplinary Commission of the Government and proceedings may be initiated by the Prosecutor General. Appeal is permitted and the decision may be challenged before the administrative court. Currently in Slovenia only one disciplinary sanction exists: the dismissal which may be imposed by the National Assembly at the proposal of the Prosecutor General. In the draft law of Slovenia new sanctions are created and the disciplinary offenses have strict definition. For certain offenses the Government will be authorized to impose such punishment as dismissal. In other cases a special disciplinary court composed of judges and prosecutors will have competence.

In Belarus, Hungary, Poland and Russia disciplinary actions are governed partly by the Labour Code, partly by other legal provisions and no judicial control is provided. In Hungary, there is a draft law on this issue.

IX. Considering the answers we have received to the points of chapter IX, we can conclude that prosecutor offices have difficulties in coping with the ever increasing case load in almost every country. Most countries follow the old managerial system and do not have knowledge of a more effective managerial approach.

The answer of Albania is encouraging from this point of view, saying that the prosecutorial organization is not able to cope with the burden of work if it applies the old style of management.

Only Slovenia has given answers in a new type of managerial spirit, saying that reorganization of units, teamwork and other managerial techniques are used..

Finally, please let me make a personal remark. When I was doing the preparatory work of our meeting and especially my report I could not help thinking about the fact that guidelines dealing exclusively with the European principles and standards regarding the role and activities of prosecutors were missing.

Let me seize this opportunity to raise the idea of the elaboration of a recommendation on the role, efficiency and impartiality of prosecutors under the auspices of the Council of Europe. As far as I know, the elaboration of such a recommendation on the role of judges and their independence is under way. No initiative to prepare a similar instrument dealing with the principles governing the prosecutorial activities has been taken yet, at least to my knowledge. I am convinced that a Council of Europe recommendation, taking into consideration the UN Guidelines on the role of prosecutors, would highly contribute to clarify the issues related to the Public Prosecution Office and would help our *sui generis* legal profession, the only one of its kind we are all dedicated to.

# TOPIC 3

# PROSECUTORIAL FUNCTIONS IN CONNECTION WITH CRIMINAL LAW: PRE-TRIAL FUNCTIONS, DISCRETIONAL POWER, TRIAL FUNCTIONS

Birgitte VESTBERG
Prosecutor (Denmark)

## Presentation of Topic 3
## in its Pan-European context

**Introduction**

The overall theme of this multilateral meeting is "The transformation of the "Prokuratura" into a body compatible with the democratic principles of law.

The first question to pose is:

Are there any democratic principles guiding the prosecutorial functions in connection with criminal law?

This question is not easy to answer. A look at the democracies in the world will - judging alone from the situation in Europe - undoubtably show a great variation in the ways in which the prosecution services are organised.

I do not pretend to give a comparative study - just let me remind you of one of the conclusions of the meeting in Vienna in May 1993:

It would be wrong to try to translate a prosecution system from one country to another.

With that in mind the next question to pose is:

Can any principles guiding prosecutorial functions be traced back to democratic constitutions?

Without another comparative study in the matter it can fairly be said, that very few constitutions contain articles on the prosecutorial functions.

This is certainly the case in the Kingdom of Denmark, and yet the constitution holds several rules from which it can be derived,

that no basic human right can be infringed but by the rule of law.

This means that basic human rights can be infringed only on conditions fixed in an act passed by a democratically elected parliament.

Human rights are now defined in the Universal Declaration of Human Rights agreed upon by the General Assembly of the United Nations on 10 December 1948. These rules will be given more attention later in the context of the European Convention on Human Rights of 4 November 1950, which has develop into a true guide to widely accepted rules on criminal justice of which a prosecution service and its powers is one part. Any country having signed the European Convention can be brought before the Human Rights Court, if the rules are not adhered to.

The Council of Europe has set up an interesting questionnaire, and as an introduction to the discussions on the replies provided by the participant countries I have been required to account for Denmark's answers to democratic requirements.

The first Danish constitution based on an elected parliament and the division of powers between the legislature, the courts and the executive came out in 1849 and from then on and still under the present constitution of 1954 the rules on criminal procedure are few, but important.

In order of appearance they are:

Criminal proceedings are oral and public
Lay judges cooperate
Detention beyond 24 hours requires a court order
Searches and seizures require a court order.

The details of these principles are set out in the Administration of Justice Act as passed by parliament and in cases of urgency the police may act without a court order on condition of making a report to be forwarded to the court.

The Administration of Justice Act also sets out the powers and obligations of the Prosecution Service, and from an overall view the prosecution is part of the executive power, subordinate to the Minister of Justice, who is responsible to Parliament.

The answers to the questionnaire show a great variety to the rules governing the subjects covered by section V, and Mr. Bocz will present the solutions.

The following will sum up the way Denmark deals with the subjects set up in the questionnaire.

A.  **The function of supervision over the legality of criminal investigation in the pre-trial phase**

Police investigates and the prosecutor can at any stage direct the investigation, give substantial orders and directives. It is the responsibility of the police and the prosecutor to secure, that the guilty are prosecuted and that the unguilty are not prosecuted.

The police is authorised to arrest a person under certain conditions set up in the law, but any detention beyond 24 hours requires a court order. Under Art. 5 in the European Convention on Human Rights everyone arrested shall promptly be brought before a court. This implies that the authorities are obliged to take action unless the arrested person is released, and it also means that action must be taken without a request from the arrested person - see the van der Sluijs, Zuideveld and Kleppe case. The European Court of Human Rights has also found, that a period of 4 days and 6 hours constituted a violation of Art. 5 Sec. 3 - see the Brogan case.

The Convention also sets up the conditions for arresting persons, but going into those details is beyond the scope of this meeting.

Unless a person is detained, which in Denmark requires a court order every 4 weeks, the case is not presented in court until the date of the trial.

Any contact with the court is dealt with by the prosecutor and counsel for the defence is mandatory in cases, where imprisonment is required by the prosecution. A legal control is thus instituted in any police action not approved previously by a court. This control is exercised either by the prosecutor who may decide to give up any measure or by the court.

In Denmark searches, seizures and interception of communications basically require a court order - in cases of urgency a report to the court on the measure. The rules are quite specific and regulated by law. The Convention in Art. 8 and the First Protocol in Art. 1 state the right for everyone to respect for his home and the entitlement to the peaceful enjoyment of one's possessions. These rights can only be set aside on conditions set up in the law.

Testimony made before a police officer or a prosecutor may not replace the witness' interrogation at the trial unless the witness is unavailable and will not become available in the forseable future. Replacement requires the court's permission and the value of the evidence may be negligible.

The principle - that evidence must orally be presented to the court at the trial - has been the rule in Denmark since 1919 and this principle is now reflected in Art. 6 Sec. 3 subsect. d:

Everyone charged with a criminal offence has the right to examine or have examined witnesses against him and to obtain the attendance and examination of witnesses on his behalf under the same conditions as witnesses against him.

Seen in context with the same Art. Sec. 1 - the right to a public hearing - makes it quite clear that evidence must be presented in court under circumstances making a cross-examination possible.

Several decisions by the European Court of Human Rights follow this line generally expressed within the scope of "FAIR TRIAL". Testimony made to the police is not inadmissible evidence, but a conviction may not be based on this alone - see the Unterpertinger case. Value to a report is added if counsel for the defence has been present with a possibility to ask questions.

These articles in the European Convention more specifically regulate Articles 9, 10, 12 and 17 of the UN Declaration:

Art. 9: No one shall be subjected to arbitrary arrest, detention or exile.

Art. 10: Everyone is entitled in full equality to a fair and public hearing ...

Art. 12: No one shall be subjected to arbitrary interference with his ... home ...

Art. 17 Sec. 2: No one shall be arbitrarily deprived of his property.

Comparing the information provided in the answers to the questionnaire part A with the requirements of the UN Declaration and the European Convention leads to the conclusion, that some attention should be given to the following issues:

1. Measures concerning basic human rights must be regulated by law

2. Court decisions are required, if basic human rights in the interest of criminal investigation are to be set aside.

**B. The power of discretion and the obligation to prosecute**

Equality of rights and independent courts are important items in democratic constitutions and also in the Declaration and in the Convention. Rules on the function of a prosecution service are few or non-existent and guidance is found in laws or regulations of individual countries. Europe is in the respect of the principle of legality and the principle of opportunity divided into two blocs with the majority following the principle of legality. Denmark follows the rule of opportunity and has done so since 1919. This principle only comes into use after the investigation has finished and established that a crime has been reported and identified a person, who has been charged with the crime.

Under Art. 6 Sec. 2 in the Convention and Art. 11 of the Declaration everyone is presumed innocent until proved guilty. This places the burden of proof with the prosecution and considering the case the prosecutor has to valuate the evidence. In case the evidence is considered insufficient to prove the guilt and there are no ways to improve the evidence, a Danish prosecutor is authorised to close the case - if there is no reasonable prospect of conviction.

"Reasonable prospect" is a vague expression and the decision rests on the assessment of a experienced prosecutor, not of the youngest member of the staff!

Rising crime rates and resources do not influence this decision - these factors might influence the speediness with which cases are forwarded, and may unfortunately also influence investigation and the discovery of unreported crimes.

Impartiality, fairness and consistency are key issues in exercising discretionary power - prior decisions of the courts serve as guiding stars. The Danish Prosecutor General issues guidelines on the handling of various categories of cases, but has so far not issued any guidelines on the balancing of evidence. No proposals to do so have been forwarded, and the necessary control is performed via a complaints system and by supervision.

Even if there is a reasonable prospect of conviction the prosecutor is authorised to waive prosecution on conditions set up in the law mainly to the benefit of persons under 18 years of age and the mentally handicapped.

The complaints- and supervisory system applies to these cases, but is used very rarely. A waiver is equivalent to a guilty verdict and is used only in cases where the accused pleads guilty. Conditions connected with a waiver require approval by the court.

The Minister of Justice is the formal head of the prosecution service and is by law obliged to decide on some cases - mainly concerning state security. Apart from libel and slander cases, where private prosecution is possible, the prosecution service has a monopoly to prosecute, and no external authority can prohibit prosecution. In theory, a private citizen can use in civil proceedings claiming prosecution, but the court is quite unlikely to uphold the contention.

The Eighth United Nations Congress on the Prevention of Crime and the Treatment of Offenders issued in 1988 "Guidelines on the Role of Prosecutors" and in countries where prosecutors are vested with discretionary powers Sec. 17 calls for guidelines to enhance fairness and consistency of approach in taking decisions in the prosecution process, including institution or waiver of prosecution. However - no indication is given as to the contents of these guidelines. The guidelines also request the Secretary-General to prepare every five years, beginning in 1993, a report on the implementation of the Guidelines. I have no opinions of what will be the contents of a report - if asked, I would advise

*if in doubt - prosecute.*

As to waivers the guidelines for Danish prosecutors are quite specific and added to this surveys of some cases are published in the yearly report from the Prosecutor General.

Judging from the replies to the questionnaire most countries adhere to the principle of legality. From a democratic point of view the one principle is not to be preferred to the other, if discretionary powers are used properly and accountably as advised at the Vienna meeting.

C.     **The role of the prosecutor in the trial phase**

The most common clause in the constitution of democratic countries is the independence of the court system. This means among other things that judges in performing their judicial duties shall not act on orders but decide the case in accordance with the law and the evidence. It can also be said that there is to be no interdependence between the court and the parties. The Declaration in Art. 10 and the Convention in Art. 6 Sec. 1 state the entitlement to

... a ... hearing by an independent and impartial tribunal ...

To the extent that criminal prosecution is instituted for an offence to an act passed by parliament the prosecutor is representing the State and in that capacity party to the case. The Guidelines on the Role of Prosecutors use in Sec. 11 the term: representative of the public interest - indicating not only the interest of the State, but also the spirit of the law which on rare occasions does not coincide with the interest of the State in a narrow sense - in a wider sense the State is always interested in correct decisions.

As stated before a Danish prosecutor is obliged by the principle of objectivity to take into account any information - even if it leads to acquittal and this also applies to the evidence presented in court. Since the prosecution has the burden of proof the prosecutor is responsible for presenting the case, (re)producing the evidence, calling the witnesses and making concluding remarks on evidence and the guilt and to suggest an appropriate sentence.

Basically counsel for defence and the prosecution have equal rights. If the prosecutor refuses to provide information or call specific witnesses, the defence can apply for the court to decide on the issue and a decision can be appealed by both parties. The dossier must be forwarded to defence as it is produced and at the latest when the indictment is served. If important new information turns up during the hearing a postponement is granted to let the party prepare the plea - this does occur particularly as defence is not obliged to reveal its line of defence in advance and since defence may turn up with new witnesses on the day of trial - this is not good form, but is not prohibited partly due to the wish to make sure that the court reaches the correct decision.

In Denmark the court takes action only on request from one of the parties. In criminal cases the important request is the indictment and the court cannot convict for facts not mentioned in the indictment. The court must apply the correct law and is not bound by the prosecutor's legal stance or that of the defence. The prosecutor is authorised to abandon the charge if the hearing excludes the possibility of a conviction - and is in fact obliged to do so under the principle of objectivity. The court is then obliged to acquit the defendant as the court is even if the defence fails to see a point of law or lack of evidence.

Once the hearing has started the court must convict or acquit and the prosecutor cannot waive prosecution at this stage.

Democratic requirements cannot be said to favour one over another of the systems described in the replies to the questionnaire. Any system following the lines mentioned below is likely to qualify as a democratic system.

1. Independent courts

2. Impartial prosecutors controlled hierarchically ultimately by a minister responsible to parliament

3. Human rights not to be set aside without a court order or court approval and on conditions set up by law

4. Legal assistance to persons risking imprisonment

5. Trial within a reasonable time.

On the part of the prosecution service it seems fair to conclude that the main object is to secure that an accused person gets a fair trial.

## TOPIC 3

# PROSECUTORIAL FUNCTIONS IN CONNECTION WITH CRIMINAL LAW: PRE-TRIAL FUNCTIONS, DISCRETIONAL POWER, TRIAL FUNCTIONS

Endre BÓCZ
Prosecutor General of Budapest (Hungary)

### General presentation of the solutions of Central and Eastern European countries

This paper is an attempt to summarise the answers given in the national reports provided by Albania, Bulgaria, Macedonia, Poland, Rumania, Russia and Slovakia - taken into account the situation in Hungary as well - to the questions of the Vth chapter of the Questionnaire.

**A.  The supervision over the legality of criminal investigations in the pre-trial phase of criminal proceedings**

The criminal procedural systems of the countries concerned - with the exception of Macedonia - were similar as they followed the same model: a special version of the traditional "continental" - or "mixed" - system, which has been developed in France at the beginning of the XIXth century.

In its framework one could find the phase of police investigation, which was considered to be an administrative activity, the phase of judicial examination, performed by the examining judge ("juge d'instruction") and the main trial, governed by the guarantees of orality, publicity, defense, etc.; This system was widespread; one of its variants had been in effect also in the Russian Empire. In the early 1920's in the USSR the authorities of the judicial examination ("organi rassledovania") were transferred from the judiciary to the Prosecutor's Office, and basically this was the model copied in the 1950's by the bulk of the Central and Eastern European countries as the "socialist way of criminal procedure". The most characteristic traits of this system were:

- the theoretically equal significance of the pre-trial and trial phases in taking evidence of what had happened and establishing the facts of the case;

- the lack of judicial control in the pre-trial stage of proceedings.

Of course, there might be some differences among the regulations of different countries; in Bulgaria and in the former USSR e.g. there was a clear-cut difference between "investigation" ("doznanie") and "examination" ("rassledovanie") with separate authorities performing each of them, while in Hungary and in some other countries the two functions were not markedly separated and as a rule, were assigned to the Police.

A further characteristic of this procedural system was that the prosecutor was entitled to inspect and control the activity of investigating/examining authorities, i.e. to instruct them, to change their decisions and evaluate the final results of their work; at the same time, the public prosecutor was - to a certain extent - in the role of the "juge d'instruction" as he had the right to decide on preliminary confinement, search and seizure, etc.

1.  Since 1989 at least the legal thinking has begun to change and the implications of the notions "rule of law", "due process of law" and "fair trial" have had their impact even on the new legislation. An explicit occurrence is a shift in division of powers among the authorities involved in criminal proceedings in favour of the court at the cost of prosecutor's rights in the pre-trial stage, in accordance with the UN Covenant on Human Rights and the European Convention on Human Rights and Fundamental Freedoms.

Out of the countries listed above, Macedonia - and perhaps Croatia and Slovenia as well - make an exception: they have always had a system which includes judicial examination during preliminary collection and examination of evidence with French-style examining judge in the leading role.

2.  According to the answers given by the countries listed, the prosecutor is independent in performing his responsibilities. Prosecutorial decisions do not need judicial approval or sanctioning even if they concern basic human rights like search-warrants or decisions ordering short-term custody.

3.  Judicial examination in the pre-trial stage does not exist in these countries - except for Macedonia. In Macedonia the division of powers between the examining judge and the prosecutor follows the traditional scheme: the prosecutor makes motions and the judge makes decisions.

4.  Detention exceeding a short period of time (in Poland and Russia e.g. 48 hours) needs - as a rule - of prosecutorial approval. In Bulgaria and Poland the arrestee - and the defence lawyer - has the right to appeal to the court. In Slovakia and in Hungary confinement exceeding 24 or 72 hours respectively may be ordered only by the court, after a hearing. In Rumania the prosecutor is entitled to order a preliminary confinement for 30 days which can be prolonged by the court.

In Russia they have a new Constitutional regulation according to which preliminary confinement over 48 hours may take place only on the written warrant of the court but this has not yet been put into effect; until the completion of the new Code on Criminal Procedure the old rules work.

As to the search and seizure warrants, they are to be issued by the prosecutor or by authorised officers of the investigating bodies (in Slovakia with the approval of the prosecutor) - except for Albania, where it is within the powers of the court. The prosecutorial decisions in Bulgaria may be complained of in court.

In Hungary search and seizure may be ordered by the Police without prosecutorial approval, but letters, telegrams and other postal parcels, before they are delivered to the addressee, may be seized upon a warrant issued by the prosecutor; without such a warrant they may only be withheld.

Wire-tapping in Albania, Hungary and Russia needs to be authorised by a court; in the rest of the countries listed it may be ordered by the prosecutor but in Bulgaria and Poland the decision of the prosecutor may be complained of in court.

5. Orality and directness are basic principles of the trial in each country concerned. The statement of the defendant or the testimony of a witness, recorded during investigation, may be used in evidence instead of hearing them in court only in extraordinary circumstances (e.g. the person in question is dead, lives abroad or is unavailable for the court for some other reason).

On the other hand: one of the characteristic features of this procedural system is that records of statements, made in the preliminary phase of the proceedings are admissible in trial. In case the oral statement of the defendant or the witness at the trial differs from the recorded one, the latter should be read in court, the difference needs explanation and it is up to the court to decide which one of them - in any - is credible.

All the reports say that the prosecutor has the right to permit the presence and participation of the defendant and/or the defence lawyer at the questioning of a witness whose recorded testimony is intended to be used instead of oral testimony in court as evidence at the trial; but such a questioning seldom occurs. Witnesses are normally questioned in the preliminary stage with a view to their testifying orally at trial. So the real problem is that ordinary witnesses are questioned by the examining authorities without participation, control or even presence of the defence because no one thinks of using the record instead of their oral testimony, but practically it may (and will) be used against him at the trial.

6. The prosecutor has full control over the activities of the examining authorities during the preliminary stage of the proceedings; he has the right to inspect their work from legal as well as from substantial point of view; he has the right to take part personally in actions, or give orders which are to be followed by the Police or other examining organs.

**B. The power of discretion and the obligation to prosecute**

1. According to the answers given all the prosecuting services follow the legality principle; that means that in case there are good reasons to believe that a criminal offence was committed the prosecutor will have to initiate criminal procedure in order

to find out what happened and who the offender was. If he finds as a result of that there is sufficient evidence with a satisfactory prospect of conviction - he will bring charges to the court.

2. Each country gave account of rising crime and insufficient resources - but only Rumania said that this may lead to shallowness in prosecutorial work; the rest of the answers refers to falling clearance rates as the result.

3. A possible interpretation of "opportunity principle" and "prosecutorial discretion" is: even in case of a satisfactorily proven offence the prosecutor is entitled to waive prosecution on grounds of absolute or relative (in comparison with other proven offences of the same offender) insignificance of a particular offence, "minima non curat praetor".

According to the answers given no such possibilities - except for Slovakia, where the prosecutor may reject prosecution on grounds that "the penalty in which the prosecution could result is negligible compared to the penalty to which the accused has already been sentenced" and Hungary, where the prosecutor may drop charges for offences which are - when compared to other offences of the same person - insignificant for the sentence.

On the other hand, as far as I know, the majority of the Central and Eastern European countries shares the doctrine of "material notion" of the criminal offence: a criminal offence is an act prohibited by law under criminal punishment <u>and being dangerous to society at the necessary level</u>. Accordingly, acts formally prohibited by law under criminal punishment but <u>not being dangerous enough to society</u> should not be regarded as criminal offences. At the same time, degree of "social dangerousness" was considered to be a matter of value-judgement; so the prosecutor who was entitled and expected to dismiss cases "if the act in question was not a criminal offence", practically did have discretional power in evaluating the "social dangerousness" of the act under examination and as a result finds it not being a criminal offence for lack of a satisfactory degree of danger to society.

4. Control of the prosecutorial activity comes from the centralised character of the Prosecuting Office: the higher standing prosecutors may give instructions, guidelines and even - in individual cases - orders to their subordinates; those interested in decisions of a prosecutor, have the right of complaint to the prosecutor's superior and the higher standing prosecutor is entitled to supervise his subordinate's decisions <u>ex officio</u> as well. Internal superintendence exists in each country; external superintendence can be found only in Rumania by the Minister of Justice - but in neither country it is possible to prohibit prosecution from outside.

5. Prosecution of offences by citizens - except for some acts like slander, libel, light bodily harm etc., as a rule, listed in law - is excluded in all the countries that answered: that means that the prosecution service has a monopoly to initiate criminal proceedings. Its refusal to prosecute may be complained or <u>within</u> the agency to the higher standing prosecutor.

6. That means that there is no counterbalance to the possible misuse of power. One has to add that in Hungary we are dealing with the preparation of a new criminal procedural code which provides for the victim to take over prosecution in case the prosecutor refuses to bring charges or abandons the case.

## C. The role of the prosecutor in the trial phase

1. As regards procedural position, procedural rights and duties, there have not been significant changes concerning the role of the prosecutor: all criminal procedural codes for long have stated that prosecution and defence enjoy equal rights in court. In this respect the public prosecutor is a party to the case. In terms of substantive interests he is a representative of the State and/or the public interest. It is worthy of mentioning that according to the answers given by Poland, in spite of the declared equality of the parties the public prosecutor's seat was for years at the table of the tribunal. About five years ago this had been changed and since then the prosecutor sits in front of the advocates' bench.

2. There are no special legal rules to oblige the prosecutor to promote the procedural possibilities of the defence. The criminal procedural code of all the countries contains provisions on the completion of a preliminary examination. The provisions are nearly the same: when the examining authority feels the examination complete it has to hand over all the files to the suspect an his/her attorney and to let them study it, and make comments which should be recorded as well as their eventual motions on further, supplementary investigations. These motions should be decided on; in case of their rejection the decision may be complained of to the prosecutor.

In Hungary the files are made in two copies: one for the court and one for the prosecutor. Under a ministerial ordinance since 1990 the examining authority has to provide - on request and for repayment of the costs - the defence with a further copy.

3. Neither planned nor implemented reforms were reported concerning the replacement of the existing inquisitorial model of trial except for such formal changes as the prosecutor stating the charges (instead of the judge) at the beginning of the trial. The planned new criminal procedural code in Hungary envisages an adversary trial with the parties presenting their cases, introducing evidence and cross-examining.

4. The court in neither country is bound by the motions and legal stances of the prosecutor (or the defence); it is independent in its decisions. The existence of accusation is the prerequisite of the court proceedings but if a charge is filed the court will be obliged to decide. The prosecutor is entitled to modify the charge, to extend it or to drop it. In case the prosecutor drops the charge the court in Hungary must dismiss the case: in the rest of the countries it may decide in merit.

## TOPIC 4

# THE ROLE OF PROSECUTORS IN THE APPLICATION OF INTERNATIONAL CRIMINAL LAW; MUTUAL ASSISTANCE IN CRIMINAL MATTERS, TRANSFER OF CRIMINAL PROCEEDINGS, EXTRADITION, etc.

Peter WILKITZKI
Ministerialrat
Ministry of Justice (Germany)


**Presentation of Topic 4
in its Pan-European context**


1.  Introduction

Aim of presentation: To identify elements of Western European (= not only German) practice and experience which might be useful for new democracies when creating new models of public prosecution services. Basic philosophy: No model solutions, just some essentials concerning the role of public prosecution in law and practice of cooperation in criminal matters. Presentation will not offer a complete "tableau", but rather a "department store" for "pick and choose" purposes, thereby following the questionnaire's structure.


2.  **Description of situation**

Europe's growing together, permeability of borders. At the same time, unfortunately, the extent, diversity and subtlety of criminal activities are also increasing at an alarming rate, thus constantly confronting the legislature, executive and judiciary of our countries with new challenges.

The rise in transboundary crime, in particular, is creating an increased need for trustful international cooperation and abandonment of exaggerated notions of sovereignty.

Special problems in Central and Eastern European countries on the one hand - on the other, experience in "classical" Council of Europe countries, which has, over the last 40 years, enabled them to achieve an exemplary level of mutual interpenetration of legal traditions and homogeneity of legal systems with outstanding cooperation in both qualitative and quantitative terms.

In the process of growing together, not only the governments but also the organs of the judiciary (the courts, public prosecution offices, sometimes the police) play a central role.

3. **Definition "International Criminal Law"**

Misunderstandings in answers to questionnaire:

The term was meant to be used in a narrow sense (only criminal law cooperation).

4. **The role of the Public Prosecution Office in extradition proceedings**

  a)    Ingoing requests:

Procedural laws in most Western European countries give the public prosecution office a stronger position in examining and deciding on the admissibility of extradition and related matters of arrest than is the case in national criminal proceedings (preparation, examination, filing of applications, supervision of custody), not however in deciding on the admissibility of extradition (always reserved to courts and governments).

  b)    The particulars of the public prosecution office's powers in extradition proceedings have to remain regulated by the <u>national</u> procedural laws.

Problems can arise insofar as contractual provisions on extradition make the admissibility of certain acts subject to <u>judicial</u> actions (for example the hearing of the extradited person in respect of the supplementary request, Article 14, para. 1 (a) of the European Convention on Extradition).

If the national laws on extradition assign such powers to the public prosecution office, incompatibilities can only be avoided if the position of the public prosecution office is judicial or similar (rule of law, independence, regulation of proceedings in conformity with judicial system).

Thus, within the framework of mutual assistance there is a particular need to regulate criminal procedure and cooperation in accordance with basic principles (human rights, due process of law, fair trial).

Complete <u>equality</u> between the public prosecution office and the court in extradition proceedings would seem doubtful, especially if the public prosecution office were given the power, within the scope of extradition, to issue warrants of arrest.

  c)    If only for practical reasons, the technical <u>execution</u> of granted extraditions cannot lie with ministries and courts, but has to lie with public prosecution offices or with police authorities supervised by them.

d) The role of the public prosecution office in _outgoing_ requests: The government can only make a request for extradition if the competent public prosecution office has issued a warrant of arrest and suggested a request for extradition.

In most countries, the Interpol red corner notice is recognized as an announcement that an extradition request will be made if the person is apprehended.

## 5. The role of the Public Prosecution Office in other legal assistance proceedings

a) _General remarks_ on the importance and forms of other areas of legal assistance; delimitation between non-contractual and contractual judicial assistance; domination of judicial assistance in Europe by European Convention on Mutual Assistance in Criminal Matters (and supplementary agreements).

To what extent are treaties on mutual assistance necessary at all? Following continental European legal traditions, most types of mutual assistance may be requested and provided also in the absence of a treaty (German experience, value of "agreed minutes" on expert's talks).

In any case, treaties are not superfluous, since by regulating prerequisites and consequences of assistance in general abstract terms they relieve countries of difficult and time-consuming negotiations of agreements and lay down calculable, clear law for both parties.

Bilateral or multilateral agreements? Western European tradition: Since the 1950ies basic precedence of multilateral treaties over bilateral treaties. Creation of a conventional network by Council of Europe (20 criminal law conventions, covering all areas of cooperation). The network merely needs to be refined by means of additional bilateral treaties in individual sectors. However, different legal traditions in other regions: Common Law states, former socialist states, preferring bilateral treaties.

Here, too, the conventional network created by the Council of Europe is gaining more and more attraction, as it enables these countries to establish treaty relations with more than 20 countries immediately. The value of multilateral treaties may be illustrated by the example of a simple mathematic sum: If all the future 40 Council of Europe member states sought to create a comprehensive network of bilateral treaties on mutual assistance, this would entail the negotiation of 780 such treaties. Thus, multilateral instruments are far more economical.

b) In what cases can a request for legal assistance _emanate_ from a judicial authority? Articles 1 and 24 of the European Convention on mutual assistance in criminal matters provide for a denomination of the authorities from which requests for legal assistance can emanate. It is a matter for each state to define this for its area. (This does not mean that a state can restrict the acceptance of such requests, if they emanate from _other_ member states, by means of its declaration regarding Article 24 of the European Convention on mutual assistance in criminal matters.)

Within the scope of the declarations regarding Article 24 of the European Convention on mutual assistance in criminal matters, almost all member states of the Convention have placed courts and public prosecution offices on an equal footing. In Western Europe, courts and public prosecution offices are equally situated under the roof of the ministries of justice; furthermore, the denomination of the public prosecution offices as judicial authorities for the purposes of Article 24 of the European Convention on mutual assistance in criminal matters includes all parts of the hierarchically-structured public prosecution office, i.e. not only the chief public prosecution office (prokuratura) but also the subordinate public prosecution offices; the particular problem of an independently-positioned chief public prosecution office beside the ministry does not arise.

(For the role of the police compare paragraph h) below.)

I will not comment on the merits of an autonomous position of the Prokuratura, but it must be examined to what extent this independence may jeopardize cooperation with states where the public prosecution service has a totally different structure.

c)  One has to distinguish between the competence for filing requests and the rules regarding the transmission channels: compare, in particular, with Article 15 (in particular para. 6) of the European Convention on mutual assistance in criminal matters.

As for the centralization or decentralization of the transmission channels, there is no uniform tendency in Western Europe.

Partly (for example in Germany) the direct channel between the judicial authorities concerned (courts and public prosecution offices, sometimes also police authorities) - notwithstanding transmission through the International Criminal Police Organisation - is striven for, partly the concentration on "central authorities" outside the diplomatic channels is favoured (for example in UN Conventions, in the United Kingdom, in Sweden; compare the exceptions valid in France even within the area of the "Schengen states").

Insofar as the direct channel is permitted, this should not be misinterpreted to mean that the central authority is excluded from the flow of information; it is a matter for the states to lay down national regulations that provide for an obligation to report to the central authority generally or in certain cases.

German model: Make the best possible use of direct channels. It is true that this can only work if there is an optimal mutual knowledge of the other system. To that end, inventories on domestic competences ("Ortsbuch") must be exchanged.

The answers to the questionnaire show that in your countries some old views still seem to have survived (centralism, bureaucracy). The application of direct channels presupposes a high degree of maturity, trust and practice, including personal contacts between practitioners.

d) <u>National legal competence</u> regarding making and executing requests for judicial assistance:

The public prosecution office's role is again to be determined by the national laws of the individual states. However, harmonization is desirable in order to avoid misdirections and delays, particularly in the case of direct transmission channels (the requesting state should know to <u>which</u> authority the request should be addressed). Possible models are (even within Germany, the regulations differ from one federal state to another): Giving general priority to the public prosecution office, as is the case in extradition proceedings, or deciding each case along the lines of the competence for corresponding acts as stipulated in the national laws of criminal procedure (e.g. orders of seizure, examinations and services of documents within the public prosecution office's responsibility, as opposed to the court's responsibility for judicial examinations and services of documents).

The fundamental differences in the procedural systems within Europe become apparent here (example: the "investigating magistrate" following the French pattern).

e) As far as the <u>presence</u> of participants in the proceedings during acts of legal assistance in the requested state is permitted, the public prosecution office of the requesting state is regularly involved; problems arise only with respect to other participants in the proceedings (defence, ancillary prosecutor).

f) Insofar as for certain offences (economic offences, organized crime) the competence of the public prosecution offices is <u>concentrated</u> in the hands of specific authorities with specialist qualifications, this does not create any problems in the case of outgoing requests, but in the case of <u>incoming</u> requests - especially those transmitted directly - it can mean that the authority which has the best grasp of matters is not reached.

g) <u>The role of the public prosecution office in the transfer of criminal proceedings</u>

The principles regarding other legal assistance proceedings that have been presented are transferable both to the "genuine" transfer of proceedings (Council of Europe Convention of 15 May 1972) and to the laying of information in connection with proceedings (Article 21 of the European Convention on mutual assistance in criminal matters).

Exception: Insofar as there are tendencies to admit direct channels, these are, in Western Europe, not always applied to such requests (example: Netherlands), so as to guarantee a central control over the loss and gain of national jurisdictional powers.

The answers to the questionnaire show that there seems to be a basic divergence between old and new Member States insofar as the role of the public prosecution service is concerned. As a general rule, the prosecutor should be given a more decisive role in such proceedings.

h) <u>The role of the police</u> in legal assistance proceedings:

The mere channelling of requests via the police is not problematic (compare paragraph b) above). However, political and dogmatic problems arise when actual authority to act on its own behalf (not just as an auxiliary organ under the instruction of public prosecution) is granted to the police in legal assistance proceedings.

Basic rule: The police will only have their own authority to act if they are competent for corresponding acts also under national procedural laws (this means that, as a rule, they will not be granted authority in the case of enforcement measures such as seizures and arrests; compare also with new forms of cooperation such as hot pursuit, transboundary observation) and if the understanding with the respective other state under international law provides for the police's competence.

Certainly, there are particular hesitations in ex-socialist countries against a more independent role of the police in international cooperation, as there is a feeling that the police is, more than bodies, "tainted" because of its role under dictatorial regimes. On the other hand, it will not be possible in the future to maintain "clinically clean" solutions. So, rather than to exclude the police totally from mutual assistance and to run the risk that a lot will be done in a "grey zone", one should try to make clear definitions of areas where the police have their own competence also in international cooperation, and to link it to substantial regulations, similar to those governing judicial assistance.

Negative effects on the functioning of judicial assistance arise from conflicts of competence between the judicial and the interior authorities <u>within</u> the respective states and from different national conceptions of the delimitation judiciary/police <u>between</u> the states (for example: different responsibilities in the preliminary proceedings, investigation proceedings, pre-trial court proceedings (if applicable), main proceedings), example: Common Law states, Scandinavia; even in the restricted area of the "Schengen States" there are considerable differencies. The spheres of responsibility and authority incumbent upon judicial (or home affairs) authorities, public prosecutors and police are defined differently and separated from one another. Areas which in State A are covered by genuine judicial assistance under the responsibility of the public prosecutor may in State B be regarded as substantive legal assistance to be effected by the police, but also as purely administrative assistance carried out by the police. Thus it is possible that in individual cases either the cooperation is considered by those two states to be governed by different instruments of international law, or that one of the States concerned might consider that several or none of those instruments are applicable, which is equally irksome. The solution can only be found in far-reaching flexibility on each side.

## 6. Final remarks

a) Problems of mutual assistance between prosecution services can be seen as a mirror of the structure and role of the prosecution service as a whole. Wherever we find theoretical or practical problems or loopholes regarding the domestic situation of prosecutors, they will inevitably have an impact on international cooperation: It can work efficiently and smoothly where this situations is satisfactory; it will fail where the domestic situation is inadequate.

b)    Exchange of experience within the competent bodies of the Council of Europe (CDPC, sub-committees "operation of conventions", "Europe in a time of change") is therefore of paramount importance. It does not only lead to a better understanding of different legal systems, but also brings about personal contacts between practitioners and scientists from all countries, going on to create friendships, which are as important in solving transfrontier problems as is the legal apparatus and which rank among the greatest signs of hope for a true, irreversible rapprochement on our continent.

## TOPIC 4

# THE ROLE OF PROSECUTORS IN THE APPLICATION OF INTERNATIONAL CRIMINAL LAW; MUTUAL ASSISTANCE IN CRIMINAL MATTERS, TRANSFER OF CRIMINAL PROCEEDINGS, EXTRADITION, etc.

**László LÁNG**
**Head of Department Prosecutor**
**Head of Criminal Investigations Department**
**of the Office of the Prosecutor General (Hungary)**

### General Presentation of the solutions of Central and Eastern European countries

Had Copernicus not summarised the astronomical pieces of knowledge accumulated up to that time in the heliocentric conception of the universe in the 16th century, then a comparison could as well be relevant today, in which the relationship of life and law would be measured to that of the Sun and the Moon trailing after it. (I am not mentioning the two kinds of light, since that is what the story is all about on this conference.)

This is not otherwise in respect to our topic, either. Unfortunately, we cannot say that the fact of crime ignoring national boundaries for a long time would have immediately led the states to recognising the necessity of a close international cooperation in criminal investigation. However, we have got beyond this at least by these days, and in my opinion, this present conference is a result and stage of the process.

The development of the Central and Eastern European countries - being similar to one another in various respects but different from that of the Western European states - created some special solutions in the so-called application of international criminal law, too. I am planning to expound these, mentioning the following in advance:

A. In all cases, the prosecution of those acts declared as criminal act by each state, via an international cooperation is meant by international criminal law.

B. The term "mutual assistance in criminal matters" is used in an expressly narrow sense - according to the Agreement of 20 April 1959, Strasbourg.

C. With regard to the description of the solutions of each country, the different interpretation of certain points of the questionnaire approved by the Council of Europe, as well as in some cases, the extremely laconic answers caused problems. For this reason, in the comparative work, I used the prevailing provisions of the agreements on mutual assistance in criminal matters related to the Central and Eastern European countries, and the administrative experience obtained in course of the concrete cooperation.

D. In this present report, only those states are meant by "Central and Eastern European countries" who gave an answer to the letter of request. As a result, the regulation of the following countries could be taken into account in course of the compilation of this present report: Albania, Republic of Byelorussia, Republic of Bulgaria, Republic of Croatia, Republic of Poland, Republic of Macedonia, Russian Federation, Rumania, Republic of Slovakia, Republic of Slovenia and of course, the Republic of Hungary.

1. **The role of the prosecutor in the application of international criminal law**

The 11 states, with a few exceptions, generally assign similar power to the prosecutor in the field of this special area of criminal investigation.

In respect to <u>extradition</u>, the prosecutorial power can be summarised as follows:

a) If another state is requesting for extradition, the court obtains the opinion of the prosecutor before making decision;

b) If another state is requested for extradition, also the prosecutor can start the extradition proceedings at the court.

The regulation of the Russian Federation is different from this, according to which the Office of the Prosecutor General of the Federation independently decides - in the investigative as well as in the trial phase of the proceedings - on both the subjects of requesting for extradition and the authorisation and performance of extradition in the cases of letters rogatory.

The solution of the Republic of Byelorussia is unknown. However, considering that the Republic of Byelorussia have not terminated the agreement on mutual assistance in criminal matters concluded between the Soviet Union and Hungary on 15 July 1958, it is probable that the solution is similar to the regulation of the Russian Federation in respect to the prosecutorial power. In short, except for the regulation of the Russian Federation, in the case of extradition, the essence of the prosecutorial power can be determined in the <u>participation in the extradition proceedings</u>.

In respect to the <u>transfer of criminal proceedings</u>, the prosecutorial power is basically twofold:

a) In the investigative phase of the proceedings, the office of the Prosecutor General of the states decides on whether to offer the prosecution to the Public Prosecutor Office of the other state, or whether to accept the prosecution offered by the other state. The bilateral agreements on mutual assistance in criminal matters in force between the Central and Eastern European states generally make it obligatory to accept the proceedings offered, and precisely regulate the reasons for the possible refusal of the acceptance (e.g. the act is not an extradition criminal act; the law of the state requested inflicts a penalty not heavier than 1 year imprisonment, etc.).

b) In our country as well as in many states of Central and Eastern Europe, the prosecutor has the possibility of initiating the transfer of the proceedings in the trial phase of the proceedings, too. In this case, however, the decision is in the hands of the Minister of Justice.

The regulation of the Russian Federation - and probably that of the Republic of Byelorussia - is different in that both in the investigative and trial phase of the proceedings, the prosecutor general decides on the subject of transfer and acceptance of criminal proceedings.

It is absolutely necessary to make the supplement to the obligatory acceptance described in point a) that the Hungarian procedural law, similarly to many states, grants the right of decision regarding the acceptance of the proceedings to the prosecutor general also in that case, if such decision is to be made in the trial phase of the proceedings offered by the other state. The reason for this is that each state regards the evidence obtained according to the rules of its own procedural law as primary. Consequently, it repeats the investigation possible in respect to the proceedings accepted, and the prosecutor shall then decide whether or not to bring the proceedings before the courts.

For the sake of completeness, I remark that the power described in point b) is very rare in the practice of the Republic of Hungary.

In respect to <u>mutual assistance in criminal matters</u>, the prosecutor has a decisive role in the investigative phase of the proceedings in most countries, which means that he independently administers the letters rogatory coming within the frame of mutual assistance in criminal matters, as well as those aiming at foreign countries.

A different regulation is to be found in the Republic of Macedonia, where the mutual assistance in criminal matters completely falls within the competence of the court. Furthermore, the regulation of the Russian Federation and probably that of the Republic of Byelorussia draws the administration of mutual assistance in criminal matters into the duties of the prosecutor both in the investigative and the trial phase of the proceedings.

2. **Are prosecutorial functions connected to international cooperation centralised at the highest organ of Public Prosecution (i.e. at the Office of the Prosecutor General) or are they decentralised?**

Comparing the prosecutorial power in those states answering the question, it can be ascertained that there are examples of the application of both kinds of solutions in connection with international criminal cooperation. In those fields of the international cooperation where the prosecutorial bodies have a right of decision on the merits (transfer of proceedings and mutual assistance in criminal matters), the authorisation of the performance of the letters rogatory is centralised; while the actual performance of procedural actions included in the letters rogatory is the task of the appointed regional Public Prosecution Office (decentralisation). This solution is followed by the Republic of Croatia, the Republic of Poland, the Republic of Slovakia, the Republic of Slovenia and the Republic of Hungary.

From the reports of Albania, the Republic of Byelorussia, the Republic of Bulgaria, the Republic of Macedonia and Rumania the conclusion can be drawn that all prosecutorial functions connected to international criminal cooperation are concentrated at the Office of the Prosecutor General.

3. **Is the direct transmission of letters rogatory and other requests permitted between judicial authorities or must letters rogatory and requests be always transmitted through diplomatic channel or the Ministry of Justice?**

In the case of Albania, the letters rogatory are transmitted through diplomatic channel in most cases. According to the law of the Republic of Bulgaria, it depends on the international agreement in what way letters rogatory are transmitted to the states requested. If the matter in the letters rogatory is prosecutorial activity, it is also possible that the Office of the Prosecutor General directly applies to the prosecutorial organisation of another state. In the Republic of Byelorussia as well as in the Russian Federation, letters rogatory are usually transmitted through diplomatic channel. However, in the case of letters rogatory transmitted to a member state of the Commonwealth of Independent States, it is also possible that the Public Prosecution Offices directly communicate with each other. The Public Prosecution Office of the Republic of Croatia communicates in the relationships of international cooperation via its Ministry of Justice. In urgent cases, however, it contacts the Ministry of Justice of the state requested via the Interpol or directly. In the Republic of Croatia, the ambition to make direct communication possible between the Public Prosecution Offices in the investigative phase of the proceedings is growing (letters rogatory serving the purpose of consultation in the case of intention aiming at initiating criminal proceedings, etc.). The Republic of Poland transmits its letters rogatory related to the transfer of criminal proceedings via the Ministry of Justice. An exception to this is its relationship with the Czech Republic, the Republic of Slovakia and the Federal Republic of Germany, in which the regional Public Prosecution Offices (of the voivodeships) have been authorised to directly contact the judicial authorities of the states mentioned. In such cases, however, the Public Prosecution Department of the Ministry of Justice has to be immediately notified. Unless otherwise provided by an international agreement, in the Republic of Macedonia, the letters rogatory are transmitted through diplomatic channel or the Ministry of Justice. In the case of Rumania, the letters rogatory are transmitted through diplomatic channel or the Ministry of Justice. With regard to a few states, including our country, it is possible that the Office of the Prosecutor General directly contacts the Office of the Prosecutor General of the state requested. The regulation of the Republic of Slovakia shows a variety of ways of communication. In the investigative phase of the proceedings, the Office of the Prosecutor General transmits the letters rogatory aiming at the performance of mutual assistance to the Office of the Prosecutor General of the state requested. At the same time, expressly in the case of mutual assistance in criminal matters, relationships have been established with the Republic of Poland, the Czech Republic, the Republic of Hungary and certain member republics of the former Soviet Union, which make it possible for the regional Public Prosecution Offices to directly contact each other. In absence of an international agreement, the diplomatic channel is chosen, or the judicial authorities of the other state are contacted via the Ministry of Justice.

### 4. The role of the police in mutual assistance in criminal matters

Considering the regulation of each country, it can be stated that the police is not a party to the international criminal cooperation. Except for the Republic of Bulgaria, in all states the police provides help in the completion of the investigative actions at the behest of the prosecutor - or court, in the case of extradition - and only within the limits the prosecutor or judge orders the police to do so in respect to the concrete case. In the regulation of the Republic of Bulgaria, the police does not participate in any way whatsoever in the application of international criminal law.

### 5. Changes in the international cooperation in criminal cases during the past few years

It has been characteristic of all Central and Eastern European countries that numerous international agreements have been ratified. In the Republic of Bulgaria, according to the Constitution of 1991, the international agreements become a part of the national law and have priority over national law. The Republic of Poland has ratified the European extradition agreement of 13 December 1957. The Republic of Slovakia has joined the European extradition agreement, the agreement on mutual assistance as well as the agreement on mutual assistance aiming at the transfer of criminal proceedings.

It has to be mentioned under "changes" that, considering the embargo involving the Federal Republic of Yugoslavia, the Republic of Macedonia could participate in the international criminal cooperation only to a limited degree. At the same time, bilateral agreements on mutual assistance have been concluded with the Republic of Croatia and the Republic of Slovenia during the past few years. All states mentioned that international relations have become more complicated, and the disintegration of the Soviet Union, Yugoslavia and Czechoslovakia constituted a serious problem.

### 6. The main problems arising from the international criminal cooperation from prosecutorial point of view

In the case of almost all countries, it causes problems that agreements on mutual assistance are lacking in the relation of many states. In Albania, this has resulted in hundreds of investigations being suspended due to the deficiencies of international criminal cooperation. The comprehensive knowledge of the systems of application of law of the European countries is lacking, too. Additionally, the Republic of Croatia mentioned the slowness of the proceedings within the international cooperation relations, the inexperience of the young prosecutors, the scarcity of special literature, and lack of translations of the foreign legal provisions. It causes serious problems for the Republic of Poland that the member states of the former Soviet Union perform the letters rogatory addressed to them delayed or not at all. The bureaucratic administration is mentioned amongst the difficulties, as well as the fact that certain states do not observe the agreements concluded. It constitutes an obstacle for the Republic of Macedonia that Greece and the Federal Republic of Yugoslavia deny the performance of mutual assistance requests of the Macedonian courts. The low level of the cooperation is the problem for Rumania, especially in the cases related to money laundering, drug traffic and organised crime. The Russian Federation has mentioned that the contact is realised through diplomatic channels, and for this reason, they do not have sufficient and up-to-date information about the fight against crime in other states, and the modern methods of scouting criminal acts and those of pursuing the committers of the crime. In the Republic of Slovakia, it is perceived that international crime is fought against mainly within national compass at present. The international agreements are useful; it seems, however, that they rather deal with the provision of national sovereignty and the untouchability of the national jurisdictional system than with the establishment of the effective international procedure of fighting against crime. The fight against crime cannot be overregulated and bureaucratic. The parties to the European agreements ratified by the Republic of Slovakia mentioned above should review their reservations related to these agreements as soon as circumstances make it possible (e.g. the reservations of Sweden in connection with Article 2, point 15 of Article 6 and point 2 of Article 16 of the European Agreement on Mutual Assistance, or the reservations of Austria regarding point 15 of Article 2 of this same agreement).

The experience of the Republic of Hungary accumulated in international criminal cooperation also confirms the problems mentioned by the states listed above. It would seem to be expedient if the Council of Europe established an office paying attention to the international agreements, their changes, and the reservations and declarations related to the agreements, which would have constant and up-to-date information on all these matters as well as on the changes in the criminal substantive and procedural law of the Central and Eastern European countries. By so doing at least the minimum requirement would be realised: that our countries would have knowledge of the fundamental rules which are in force in the state in question in course of the concrete cooperation. It would be extremely useful if more information was available on the agencies of the Russian Federation administering mutual assistance in criminal matters; and the direct communication of the prosecutors involved in international criminal cooperation could be realised in Central and Eastern Europe at all. Those committing the crime are beyond contacting each other for a long time. Without intending to dramatise the situation, we are approaching the eleventh hour. For this reason, the establishment of close and direct relations is hardly to be postponed any further.

> **TOPIC 5**
>
> **FUNCTIONS OF THE PUBLIC PROSECUTOR'S OFFICE IN CONNECTION WITH CIVIL LITIGATIONS AND ITS EXTRA JUDICIAL FUNCTIONS**
>
> Christian PAUL-LOUBIERE
> Magistrat at the
> Tribunal de Grande Instance of Paris
> Chargé des Travaux dirigés at the
> University of Paris Panthéon-Sorbonne (France)

**Presentation of Topic 5
in its Pan-European context**

INTRODUCTION

Title VIII of the law of 16 and 24 August 1790, enacted when France was in the throes of the Revolution, defines the Office of the Attorney General thus:

> "... a specific legal service (magistrature) established in certain jurisdictions in order to represent society as a whole and, in its name, to ensure in the courts the application of the laws aimed at protecting order in general, and the enforcement of judgments."

This definition was supplemented some years later by PORTALIS, a member of the famous Drafting Commission for the Civil Code of 1804, in the following terms:

> "The Office of the Attorney General (Ministère Public) is a legal institution: it regulates judicial practice, offers help and solace to the weak and oppressed and is a formidable prosecutor of the wicked. Finally, it safeguards the general interest and in doing so acts as a representative to the body of society."

The unity, indivisibility and above all independence - from the courts, as well as from political power - which the Office of the Attorney General displays are crucial in enabling it to fulfil its key role in our democratic institutions.

As distinct from its well-known prosecuting functions in criminal matters, where the Attorney General intervenes to protect the general interest, the Office of the Attorney General has an equally important role in civil matters.

The Attorney General may take action in a judicial or extra-judicial context, and as joined party or as principal party, to guarantee the protection of the general interest and of the interests of individuals and to ensure that any non-compliance with law is punished by the courts.

I shall not discuss at this point the law relating to civil liberties in the context of the impact of the Office of the Attorney General on our democratic institutions, because in civil litigation the Office of the Attorney General only intervenes incidentally as a direct defender of civil liberties.

This is because positive law in France does not grant judges direct control over constitutional legality (civil liberties having acquired constitutional value in the hierarchy of juridical norms, as recalled in the preambles to the Constitutions of 1946 and 1958). This differs from the situation in the USA, where a special statute can be used in order to control constitutional legality, and in Germany, where a special statute or legal proceedings can be used similarly.

The Constitutional Court alone exercises effective control of a preventive nature over the constitutionality of legislation.

Violations of civil liberties are sometimes dealt with administratively, mainly by the State Council (Conseil d'Etat) and the Jurisdiction Court (Tribunal des Conflits), which deal with conflicts between the authorities and individuals. Violations are also dealt with judicially, especially in criminal cases, by the Criminal Division of the Court of Cassation, when they relate to relations between individuals and the protection of their personal liberties (libertés privées).

This distinction originates from the law of 16 and 24 August 1790, enacted during the Revolution, which you will recall, prohibits the judiciary from interfering in the decisions of the executive, in accordance with the doctrine of separation of powers.

In criminal cases, the Office of the Attorney General plays an important role in defending civil liberties. In civil cases, however, it refers matters to the judges or suggests to them that specific violations of the right to property, marriage or privacy, for example, might be sanctioned.

With regard to civil matters, the Office of the Attorney General has a wide sphere of action, but an exhaustive analysis of its various aspects is beyond the ambit of this presentation.

In my opinion it is more important to show in what respects the Office of the Attorney General performs a regulatory function within democratic institutions in France.

The Office of the Attorney General is guided by a constant concern to maintain a proper balance between the general interest (of society as a whole) and individual interests, which a liberal society has a responsibility to protect.

This balance is attained either through a compromise between aspirations which are often not easy to reconcile, or through good will on all sides.

The delicate nature of the mission of the Office of the Attorney General thus becomes clear: to act as arbitrator at the point in our institutions where the paths of law and of its enforcement cross, where government and citizen meet, thus ensuring the observance of the Social Contract, which is the cornerstone of our democracy.

That is why my presentation will deal with the functions of the Office of the Attorney General in civil matters with respect to its two fundamental aims

* firstly the protection of the general interest and the protection of the interest of individuals;

* and secondly the control and sanctions necessary for the amelioration of social cohesion.

## I. THE PROTECTIVE ROLE OF THE OFFICE OF THE ATTORNEY GENERAL

In order to maintain a proper balance between the interests of individuals and the general interest, the Office of the Attorney General performs its protective role essentially in the courts. The law of 16 and 24 August 1790 state:

> "In civil matters the King's Commissioners (Commissaires du Roi) shall exercise their functions not by taking cases to the courts, but by making submissions (réquisitions) in cases already referred to the judges".

The law of 20 April 1810 adds:

> "In civil proceedings the Office of the Attorney General shall commence proceedings on its own initiative in cases specified by the law ..." (Article 46)

In these early texts it is already possible to see the distinction between the Office of the Attorney General acting as joined party and the Office of the Attorney General as principal party, which was taken up again in Article 421 of the New Code of Civil Procedure of 1975, now in force.

This distinction can also be found in the legal prerogatives of the Attorney General, both in the field of the protection of personal interests and in that of the protection of the general interest.

## A. PROTECTION OF THE PERSONAL INTERESTS

### 1. The Office of the Attorney General acting proprio motu

Here the Office of the Attorney General intervenes following the inability of certain individuals to act, when they fail to exercise their rights either because they are physically unable to do so or because they lack the necessary understanding.

a. Protection in cases of absence and disappearance

Article 117 of the Civil Code provides that "The Office of the Attorney General has a special duty to look after the affairs of persons presumed to be absent in order to safeguard their interests and that" that "it has a say in all applications concerning such persons" and above all that it may on its own initiative request the application or modification of the measures provided for in Title IV relating to absentees.

Thus the Attorney General may order measures to protect and manage an absentee's financial affairs and property, starting with an application to the guardianship judge (Juge des Tutelles) to establish the presumption of absence. Article 1063 of the New Code of Civil Procedure specifies that "the application shall be lodged, investigated and decided according to the rules governing the guardianship of minors".

The Attorney General may then ask the court to make a declaration of absence. If the absentee comes back or if his or her existence is subsequently proven, the Office of the Attorney General may make an application to have the judgment set aside.

In cases of disappearance, Article 88 of the Civil Code lays down that a declaration of death may be issued by the court following a request from the Office of the Attorney General in respect of any person who has disappeared in life-threatening circumstances and whose body cannot be found.

The declaratory judgment then takes the place of a death certificate and is entered in the margin of the civil register. This has the effect of opening up the succession. Article 92 lays down that, should the person declared deceased reappear, the Office of the Attorney General may apply to have the declaratory judgment set aside.

In matters of succession, the Office of the Attorney General intervenes in order to have the official seals placed or removed after a death, to carry out an inventory of the estate and to appoint an administrator when this has not already been done (Article 820 of the Civil Code).

By these means the Office of the Attorney General protects the interests both of existing heirs and of beneficiaries unknown or who have not yet come forward for a share of the estate.

The Office of the Attorney General may act in the same way in order to protect the property of a person of full age who is under legal protection, when his or her property may be put at risk (Article 1233 of the New Code of Civil Procedure).

b.   Protection in cases of incapacity

Persons of full age lacking legal capacity (incapables majeurs) enjoy the special protection of the Office of the Attorney General, which plays an important role in cases of guardianship (tutelle), supervision (curatelle) or judicial protection (sauvegarde de justice), (Articles 492-2, 493 and 509 of the Civil Code).

The Attorney General may attend the interviews conducted by the guardianship judge with the person to be protected, after the judge has duly notified him of the holding of the hearing. The Attorney General may also request information, which is usually obtained through social enquiries or the checking of evidence.

Notification of the procedure to the Office of the Attorney General is always compulsory (Articles 1241 to 1261 of the New Code of Civil Procedure).

The Office of the Attorney General may also take steps to have set aside, either wholly or in part legal transactions performed by persons lacking capacity (Articles 510-3 of the Civil Code).

In the same way, under the system of judicial protection (sauvegarde de justice), the Office of the Attorney General may make an application to a judge for the dismissal of an administrator appointed by the court to manage the financial affairs and property of a protected adult (Article 491-3 of the Civil Code).

In the case of a person of unsound mind confined to an institution, Article L352 of the Public Health Code grants the Attorney General the authority to make an application for a private hearing in the Regional Court for the appointment of an administrator (curateur) responsible for managing the financial affairs and the property of the person concerned and to safeguard his or her interests.

The second paragraph of Article L351 of the Public Health Code grants the Office of the Attorney General, where appropriate, the power to apply for the immediate discharge or release of a person of unsound mind.

Finally, Articles L355-4 et seq. of the Public Health Code define the role of the Attorney General with respect to the placing of dangerous alcoholics.

The Office of the Attorney General also pays considerable attention to the situation of minors, under the following headings:

-   parental authority

-   guardianship (tutelle)

- adoption

- war orphans (pupilles de la nation)

- the establishment of paternity with respect to children of unmarried parents.

<u>Parental authority</u>

The Attorney General may make an application for educational measures (assistance éducative) to the Children's Judge (Article 375 of the Civil Code).

In an emergency situation brought to his attention as a result, inter alia, of a police investigation of a crime, the Attorney General has the power under Article 375 (5) to arrange for a minor to be placed in a reception centre or observation centre immediately.

The Attorney General must refer the case within 8 days to a judge competent to reach a decision in the best interests of the minor.

Thus the initial decision leading to the minor's removal from parental authority is taken by the Office of the Attorney General.

The Attorney General observes the educational measures procedure and may make an application to the judge for reports on the minor's health, personality or financial situation (Article 1183 paragraph 2 of the New Code of Civil Procedure).

In matters relating to the establishment of paternity in cases of children of unmarried parents, the Attorney General may require the Family Judge (Juge des Affaires Familiales) to alter the conditions under which parental authority is exercised (Article 374 of the Civil Code in the wording derived from the law of 8 January 1993).

The Office of the Attorney General exercises the same prerogative in divorce proceedings under Article 289.

The Office of the Attorney General may commence proceedings in the Regional Court for an order removing partially withdrawing, or delegating, parental authority.

The decision to deprive parents of their authority is taken with due regard to the financial and personal circumstances of the parents. The decision can include all minors who were already born at the time of the order.

If parental authority is subsequently reinstated, the Office of the Attorney General may still make an application for educational measures, should this be necessary (second paragraph of Article 380 of the Civil Code).

In the special circumstances governed by Article 27 of the Decree of 14 January 1974, when the physical well being of a child could be at risk through the refusal of a legal guardian to grant permission to carry out certain medical procedures, or when such permission cannot be obtained, the doctor in charge may apply to the Attorney General to grant authorisation to the medical services to carry out the relevant medical emergency procedure.

### Guardianship (tutelle)

The Office of the Attorney General may refer a case to the Guardianship Judge (Juge des Tutelles) with a view to instituting guardianship proceedings (Article 391 of the Civil Code) and may intervene at any stage in these proceedings as it does in cases of guardianship of persons of full age lacking legal capacity, with due regard to the special role played by the Family Council (Conseil de Famille), and with reference to Articles 416, 446 and 447 of the Civil Code.

### Adoption

Applications for adoption must be submitted to the Attorney General, who refers them to the court after obtaining the necessary information through social and police enquiries. The information so obtained is equally useful to the Office of the Attorney General giving an opinion and to the court deciding the case.

### War orphans (pupilles de la nation)

Article 467 of the Code dealing with the pensions of invalids and the victims of war lays down that, in the absence of a legal guardian, the Attorney General himself must make the application for a child who is a victim of war to be taken into the care of the State.

### Establishment of paternity with respect to a child of unmarried parents

The Office of the Attorney General has the power to contest the establishment of paternity with respect to a child of unmarried parents if the evidence found in any of the civil status documents make the establishment of paternity pronounced in accordance with the procedures in Article 339 of the Civil Code seem improbable.

An example of such evidence forming an intrinsic part of a civil status document can be found in a case to have set aside the establishment of paternity in respect of a child by a transsexual (decision of the Regional Court of MARSEILLE on 27 January 1982 JCP 83 II, 20028).

The various circumstances we have just described under which the Office of the Attorney General may act ex proprio motu as a principal party are laid down mostly in the Civil Code but also, as we have seen, in other specific texts. They correspond to the category of "cases specified in the law" within the meaning of Article 422 of the New Code of Civil Procedure. As stated earlier, this text defines the power of Office of the Attorney General to act ex proprio motu in civil disputes.

As a party to the proceedings, the Office of the Attorney General has access to all forms of redress, mainly in the shape of appeals on points of fact and appeals on points of law . When the Attorney General acts as joined party, the means of obtaining redress are reduced.

b.  The major consultative role of the Office of the Attorney General

Article 424 of the New Code of Civil Procedure states:

"The Attorney General's Office shall act as joined party when it intervenes to give its opinion on the application of the law in a case of which it is notified."

The two important words in this text are "opinion" and "communicable". That is because, as a joined party, the Office of the Attorney General remains extraneous to the proceedings and only gives its opinion, by way of submissions, as to how the case might be resolved in the general interest.

Consequently, the Office of the Attorney General is not, in this instance, a true party to the proceedings.

Articles 425, 426 and 427 of the New Code of Civil Procedure specify the different instances of notification of the Office of the Attorney General: notification may be statutory, discretionary or judicial.

With respect to the protection of the interests of individuals, only statutory notification under Article 425 is of any relevance.

The first paragraph of Article 425 lays down that the Office of the Attorney General must be notified of cases relating to lawful descent, the administration of the guardianship of minors, and the commencement of, or changes, in the guardianship of persons of full age.

The law therefore requires notification of all procedures relating to the matters above and not introduced proprio motu by the Office of the Attorney General.

A case is not prepared and debated until the Office of the Attorney General has given its opinion.

In the same way as when it acts ex proprio motu, the Office of the Attorney General has a role to play here in the protection of the interests of certain categories of persons.

But some clarification is called for.

Notification of the Office of the Attorney General is also compulsory in matters of adoption since Article 798 of the New Code of Civil Procedure states that the Office of the Attorney General must be notified of non-contentious cases, which include adoption proceedings.

The same rule applies to proceedings relating to the abandonment of a child (Article 1161 of the NCCP).

Finally, the adoption of a war orphan is also subject to the opinion given by the Office of the Attorney General, as required under Article L468 of the Code of Military Invalidity Pensions.

Article 1180 of the New Code of Civil Procedure states that, in matters of parental authority, applications pursuant to Article 371-4 of the Civil Code must only be decided after the opinion of the Office of the Attorney General has been given. This text applies, inter alia, to decisions concerning the personal relationship of a child with his or her grand-parents, or with others (in terms of rights of access, for example). The matter is one of public policy and hence mandatory, consequently the Court of Cassation was able to set aside some rulings of the Appeal Court on the grounds that they had been given without prior notification of the Office of the Attorney General.

The Attorney General must also be heard in connection with joint declarations relating to parental authority over a child, (Article 374 of the Civil Code).

With respect to the guardianship (tutelle) and supervision (curatelle) of persons of full age, the Office of the Attorney General must be notified of all cases relating to the commencement of these protection regimes or changes in their conditions (Article 425 of the New Code of Civil Procedure).

Finally, in cases concerning relations between spouses, Articles 1286 to 1289 of the New Code of Civil Procedure state that judgments empowering one spouse to execute alone a legal instrument which normally requires the co-operation or consent of the other spouse, or granting one spouse the right to represent the other generally (Articles 217 or 219 of the Civil Code), as well as judgments transferring powers under the matrimonial regime from one spouse to the other (Article 1426) may not be delivered unless the Office of the Attorney General has first been notified.

The different texts which provide for notification of the Office of the Attorney General and which are not mentioned in the first paragraph of Article 425 of the Civil

Code come under the third paragraph of the same article, which stipulates that the Office of the Attorney General must be notified in all cases in which it has a legal duty to submit observations.

As a joined party to the proceedings, the Office of the Attorney General plays a purely consultative role and gives impartial advice by stressing points of facts or points of law which may have an effect on the decision of the court.

As it is not fully a party to the proceedings, the Office of the Attorney General may not appeal on points of fact or on points of law - it may only appeal in the interests of the law.

Thus, by way of compulsory notification - which applies generally to all cases referred to the Court of Cassation - the Office of the Attorney General plays a crucial role in the evolution and the unification of French law in relation to the protection of the interests of individuals, as well as the protection of the general interest. It can therefore be said that the Office of the Attorney General has a major consultative role.

**B.     THE PROTECTION OF THE GENERAL INTEREST**

In order to achieve the protection of the general interest in the courts, the Office of the Attorney General commences proceedings or intervenes at particular points in the proceedings.

**1.      The Office of the Attorney General acting proprio motu**

In civil matters, the action taken by the Office of the Attorney General to protect the common interest may be placed, broadly speaking, under the following three headings: preserving harmonious socio-cultural environment, maintaining healthy economic, financial and commercial markets, and safeguarding public policy and public order.

a.      Preserving a harmonious socio-cultural environment

The Office of the Attorney General plays a role in protecting the identity of the French people and French nationals in the following way:

*       French nationality can be acquired by birth on French territory (jus soli), by descent (jus sanguini) or by naturalisation, all three being major determinants of assimilation into French culture.

*       The system of civil status registration (état civil) which lays down in a manner that might almost be described as sacrosanct, the main components of each national's identity, namely his or her descent and name.

The Nationality Code and the New Code of Civil Procedure make the Office of the Attorney General the main protagonist in procedures relating to nationality.

Article 129 of the Nationality Code provides in this respect:

"Any person has the right to act in order to determine whether he (or she) has French nationality. The Attorney General has the same right in relation to any person. He (or she) acts as the defendant in any action to obtain a declaration of nationality. The Office of the Attorney General shall be involved whenever a question relating to nationality is raised in the course of proceedings in a court empowered to decide such matters."

In addition, Article 1040 of the New Code of Civil Procedure says:

"Any action with the principal aim of obtaining a declaration as to whether a person has French nationality or not shall be brought by the Office of the Attorney General, or against it."

The question of nationality is a preliminary point of law which comes under the exclusive competence of the Regional Court and an application must be submitted to the Attorney General so that he (or she) may be party to the proceedings (Article 1042 of the New Code of Civil Procedure).

In matters of nationality, the Office of the Attorney General acting as principal party may oppose an application on grounds of descent (Article 197 of the Civil Code and Court of Cassation, 1st Civil Division 8 January 1974: DS 1975, 160, page 162).

The Office of the Attorney General also acts proprio motu in the interest of the safekeeping of the civil status register and the correctness of its entries. Article 99 of the Civil Code lays down that the Attorney General may submit an application to the court for the correction of entries or for declaratory judgments or judgments supplementing civil status documents.

The law requires the Attorney General to act when an error or omission relates to the main entry or decision taking its place, or when it relates to a person without any means (this last case is governed by Article 3 of the law of 10 December 1850). Finally, the Attorney General may arrange for the correction of purely factual errors and omissions by giving instructions to that effect to the keepers of the civil status registers.

The Attorney General must, under the law of 20 November 1919, initiate the proceedings for contesting a name.

b.  Maintaining a healthy economic, financial and commercial climate

The Office of the Attorney General has played an increasing role in the settlement of liabilities by companies and other legal persons. The evolution of the law in France shows that the role of the Office of the Attorney General in this area has increased and that as a result there has been greater protection of the general interest, through a determination to make business and trade sounder (for example, by encouraging the commencement of bankruptcy proceedings as soon as a trader becomes insolvent).

The laws of 10 July 1970, 15 October 1981 and 25 January 1985 have considerably strengthened the presence of the Office of the Attorney General in the Commercial Courts (Tribunaux de Commerce).

At the same time, in contrast with the law of 13 July 1967, which clearly showed the legislator's will to protect the interests of the creditors of businesses, some of the measures contained in the law of 25 January 1985 aim at a greater protection of financially viable businesses and at the protection of a healthy economic environment, to the detriment of creditors. This much is clear firstly from the conditions laid down in Article 40, which are favourable to creditors inasmuch as they apply when creditors take part in the business rescue plan, and secondly from the suspension in such cases of individual debt recovery prosecutions.

The new law of 1994, which is not yet implemented, provides for more precise developments and demonstrates the legislator's will to protect above all the interests of the market at the expense of businesses, even when they are viable.

In its role as protector of the economic and commercial environment and throughout the bankruptcy procedure, the Office of the Attorney General has considerable powers. The Office of the Attorney General acts in three main ways:

* firstly, it ensures the observance of the law

* secondly, it checks the occupational standards of traders

* and thirdly it intervenes to defend public policy and the economy.

Its powers are extensive and manifold. For example, the Office of the Attorney General may apply for the commencement of a procedure of rehabilitation or one of liquidation, it may ask for the date of cessation of payments to be fixed or postponed, and it may request the full application of the general regime to firms normally coming under the "simplified procedure". It may also request that the agencies involved in the procedure be replaced, that their tasks be changed, or that measures taken by them be set aside.

Within the framework of the business rescue plan, the Office of the Attorney General may make an application for a change of managers, order them to make good the deficiency of assets, and apply to the court for the assessment of their personal assets, when applicable.

The Attorney General may intervene in relation to the termination of a commercial lease (location-gérance), or in relation to the prolongation of a period of observation, or to authorise the commencement or termination of a lease.

As provided in the law of 25 January 1985, the Office of the Attorney General acting as the principal party may appeal; in fact, the law provides that it may even appeal when it is not a party to the proceedings.

c.   Safeguarding public policy

Following a long judicial controversy throughout the nineteenth century, the judgment delivered on 25 May 1869 (Dalloz Périodique 69-1-413) by the State Council (Chambre des Requêtes) stated clearly that the Office of the Attorney General may act proprio motu as principal party in all circumstances when public policy is directly affected.

The case of 17 December 1913 defined the limits of intervention for the Office of the Attorney General by specifying that the right to act can only be justified in circumstances where public policy matters are at issue, and where there is no danger of competing interests being jeopardised.

This articulation of the role of the Office of the Attorney General confirms its responsibility in preserving the balance between the common interest and the interests of individuals.

Finally, Article 423 of the New Code of Civil Procedure lays down:

"It [The Office of the Attorney General] shall take action to defend public policy in circumstances when the latter is adversely affected."

In 1886 the State Council (Chambre des Requêtes) defined public policy thus:

"The political, social, economic and moral organisation of a country as conceived by the legislator acting as representative of the public conscience and guardian of the general interest.'In 1950 the Appeal Court of NANCY supplemented this definition with the following words:

"By public policy we do not mean solely measures concerning public order (paix publique) or the relations in which the State or a public activity is involved; public policy also includes the protection of people lacing legal capacity and the protection of poor people.'

However, the defence of public policy has its limits in that it must not adversely affect a competing interest (as defined in the judgment of 1913).

On 16 April 1969, the Court of COLMAR dismissed an action brought by the Office of the Attorney General contesting a decision in affiliation proceedings because it was against the interests of the child, and liable to harm the peace of mind and honour of the family in question".

The Office of the Attorney General may act on its own initiative not only in matters of descent and in annulments of marriage, but also in order to issue a writ against a landlord who is in breach of his obligation to notify empty property to the authorities in the general interest, or in order to stop the fraudulent activities of a building society (société coopérative de reconstruction).

The placement of dangerous alcoholics, which is decided on the initiative of the Office of the Attorney General, also comes under public policy (Article L 355-4 et seq. of the Public Health Code).

## 2. The Office of the Attorney General acting as joined party

Article 125 (2) of the Civil Code stipulates that the Office of the Attorney General must be notified in the following cases: <u>bankruptcy</u>, stay of proceedings, settlement of debts and rehabilitation or liquidation procedures involving corporate bodies, traders and craftsmen.

Within the framework of the rules laid down in the law of 25 January 1985 and of its implementing decree of 27 December 1985, the Office of the Attorney General may, acting as a joined party, play an important role in ensuring the soundness of the economy, namely trade and industry.

The intervention of the Office of the Attorney General coincides with the commencement of the business rescue procedure. When such a case comes before the court, the president of the court gives the Attorney General a note setting out the reasons for bringing the case to court. The Office of the Attorney General is also notified of the order opening the procedure (Articles 8 and 19 of the Decree).

The court then decides whether the period of observation should be prolonged, but only after considering the opinion of the Attorney General, who is notified of the final decision (Article 20 of the Decree).

Reports from the office of the administrator appointed and from the office of the creditors' legal representative, on the progress of the business with regard to meeting its liabilities are sent to the Attorney General, as are reports relating to the implementation of the plan, transfer offers etc.

When the court rules that a liquidation should take place, the Attorney General is kept informed of the process until the proceedings are concluded by the court.

Article 1041 of the New Code of Civil Procedure provides that when an ordinary court deals in the course of proceedings with <u>a question of nationality</u>, this being a preliminary question which is not within its competence, the Office of the Attorney General must be notified of this matter.

Finally, Article 1051 of the New Code of Civil Procedure states that <u>in matters relating to correction of entries in the civil status register</u>, the application for correction is lodged, investigated and decided as a non-contentious matter, notification of the Office of the Attorney General being obligatory in such cases.

To be more precise with regard to the functions of the Office of the Attorney General when it acts as a joined party to proceedings, the observations it submits to the court may reflect particular concerns. As its interventions are only "accessory" to the proceedings, the Office of the Attorney General has a duty to respect the principle of immutability of the subject matter of the proceedings, meaning that the subject matter is fixed by the parties and that judges must work within these limits. The Office of the Attorney General must not broaden the proceedings, and in particular it must not put forward claims which the litigants themselves would not have put forward.

However, the importance of the contribution of the Office of the Attorney General in the proceedings lies in the fact that it may bring to the proceedings all documents and information dealing with facts or points of law and capable of contributing to a settlement of the dispute.

As a guarantor of public policy and a protector of the general interest, the Office of the Attorney General also has a duty to draw to the attention of the judges any relevant public policy issues, even if these extend beyond the frame of the civil proceedings (here we should note a relaxation of the principle of the immutability of the subject matter of litigation, which parallels the judge's power to introduce issues of public policy into the proceedings).

The failure to notify the Office of the Attorney General of a case when notification is mandatory, or when it is discretionary and has been requested by the Office of the Attorney General, results in automatic setting aside of the decision of the court.

The initiative for having a decision set aside lies with the parties. It should be noted that when notification of the Office of the Attorney General has been prescribed in the general interest, the party having lost the case may, since it is in his interest, apply to have the decision set aside. When notification is required in the interest of one of the parties, only the party concerned, if he has lost the case, may apply for the setting aside of the decision on the ground of failure to notify.

The application for the judgment to be set aside may be referred either to the Appeal Court on points of fact, or to the Court of Cassation on points of law on points of law when the judgment is one of last resort.

The functions of the Office of the Attorney General relating to the protection of individual interests and of public policy are performed mostly in the judicial setting, unlike its function of oversight (contrôle), where rather than acting as an independent legal authority, it acts more as a legal service for the government and has responsibility for the overall legality of the system.

## II. THE SUPERVISORY ROLE OF THE OFFICE OF THE ATTORNEY GENERAL

This role is essentially administrative, and interventions take place in a non-judicial setting, in the general interest.

An exception to this is the role of the Office of the Attorney General in the general review of legality. The Attorney General may decide to file an application for retrial (pourvoi en Cassation dans l'intérêt de la loi) under Article 17 of the law of 3 July 1967 or to bring an action against a decision by which the courts have exceeded their jurisdiction (pourvoi pour excès de pouvoir) under Article 18 of the same law.

Its supervisory powers enable the Attorney General to detect infringements of the rules and subsequently refer them to the courts. Its main area of supervision remains the administration of justice,in its widest sense, although it also carries out effective supervision of institutions and professions which play a fundamental role in the maintenance of socio-economic equilibrium.

## A. SUPERVISION RELATING TO THE ADMINISTRATION OF JUSTICE

Here, the Office of the Attorney General is concerned with enhancing the effectiveness and integrity of the judiciary. For this reason, it supervises officers of the court, who hold posts which sometimes involve the exercise of public authority, facilitates access to justice and sees to the fairness of proceedings.

### 1. Overseeing the officers of the court

The supervisory duties of the Attorney General extend to public legal officers (officiers publics), legal officers (officiers ministériels), advocates (avocats), court registrars (greffiers) in Commercial Courts and Industrial Tribunals, court experts, certain categories of public servants, and civil status registrars (officiers d'état civil).

#### a. Supervision of public legal officers and legal officers

Notaries (notaires), bailiffs (huissiers de justice), principal registrars of the Commercial Courts (greffiers en chef des tribunaux de commerce), auctioneers (commissaires priseurs) and advocate to the council (avocats au conseil) are all public legal officers.

Their interventions have the effect of authenticating the documents they process.

As a result these documents become authentic official documents.

These occupations enjoy a monopolistic position in the administration of justice. In return, they demand a high degree of competence, probity and honesty.

Because of this requirement, the authorities oversee the occupational structure and the activities of public legal officers and of legal officers.

The Office of the Attorney General controls the entry into these occupations, which are part of the public service and governed by acts which fall within the government's prerogative and which cannot be questioned by legal proceedings (acte de gouvernement). The characteristics of such occupations may not, therefore, be modified by the postholders.

Only the authorities may award or withdraw an office which involves the exercise of public authority. The Office of the Attorney General therefore applies rigorous checks in relation to the assignment of offices: the candidate has to produce proof of his or her civil status and qualifications and information on the financial conditions attached to the assignment.

The completed application file, once successfully vetted (décision d'admittur) by a court acting on behalf of the Office of the Attorney General, is then transmitted to the Ministry of Justice (Chancellerie).

The Office of the Attorney General also supervises the creation, transfer and withdrawal of offices and the setting up of civil-law professional partnerships (société civile professionnelle) to run an office. <u>Supervision of professional activity</u> by the Office of the Attorney General takes the form of audits carried out by members of the particular profession, who have been delegated this task by one of the professional organisations (Departmental Association of Bailiffs, Notaries, etc.

The Office of the Attorney General also keeps under review the scale of charges used by bailiffs and notaries. Remuneration follows strict rules and is determined by decree.

On the initiative of the Office of the Attorney General, the failure to abide by professional rules leads to disciplinary proceedings as regulated by the order of 28 June 1945 (amended by the law of 25 July 1973) and by the decree of 28 December 1973.

Article 10 of the Order of 1945 provides:

"The Attorney General shall bring disciplinary proceedings before the Regional Court".

When disciplinary proceedings are lodged by the disciplinary committee (chambre de discipline) governing the profession as result of an application made by its president, the Office of the Attorney General must be notified of the proceedings.

Disciplinary action against the registrars of the Commercial Courts is governed by the law of 16 July 1987.

The decisions of the Regional Court in disciplinary matters may be referred to the Appeal Court by the Office of the Attorney General.

b.  <u>Supervision of the legal and para-legal professions</u>

The Office of the Attorney General carries out equally effective supervision of legal officers such as advocates, administrators appointed by the courts, official liquidators, auditors and experts.

It is worth noting, with respect to access to the profession of advocate, that the decision to place a new member on the Roll of the Bar is taken by the Bar Council

(Conseil de l'Ordre), the body with overall responsibility for the Bar attached to a Regional Court (Tribunal de Grande Instance), usually at the level of each "département".

The Attorney General may refer decisions taken by the Bar Council to the Appeal Court so that they can be challenged.

The Bar Council takes decisions on disciplinary matters, either proprio motu or on the initiative of the Office of the Attorney General attached to the Appeal Court (law of 31 December 1971 governing the profession of advocate).

The Attorney General ensures the enforcement of disciplinary sanctions and of temporary exclusion from practice, as necessary.

## 2. Supervision of the administration of justice

The Office of the Attorney General has a duty to oversee the elections of judges to Industrial Tribunals and to the Commercial Courts and to ensure their conformity with the rules. The Office of the Attorney General examines official records relating to the elections in order to ascertain whether there are any grounds for complaint).

The New Code of Civil Procedure grants the Office of the Attorney General certain duties regarding the service of judicial documents on litigants whose domicile is abroad or is unknown (see Articles 659 and 684 of the New Code of Civil Procedure).

The Office of the Attorney General also has a duty to check the official records of judgments and to point out any mistakes contained therein.

The Office of the Attorney General may thus make an application to the court for the correction of a factual error. Finally, the Office of the Attorney General intervenes in matters relating to legal aid, by appealing against the decisions of the legal aid boards appointed by the courts and Appeal Courts.

Through the powers conferred on it, the Office of the Attorney General can therefore, in virtue of its functions, may make justice accessible to persons lacking means, which adds a social element to its supervisory role.

## B. SUPERVISION OF INSTITUTIONS OR ACTIVITIES WITH A SOCIO-ECONOMIC PURPOSE

The Office of the Attorney General performs a multi-faceted supervisory role which concerns different areas of social life.

*Marriage and civil status:* marriage is the basic unit in our society. Although its prevalence is declining somewhat because of a noticeable trend towards cohabitation between unmarried partners, it remains nevertheless an institution of particular concern to the Office of the Attorney General.

The Office of the Attorney General may act to annul a marriage or to oppose its celebration when public policy is adversely affected (Article 184 of the Civil Code). Furthermore, it may grant age dispensations (Article 145) or dispensations relating to publication or the requirement for a medical certificates (Article 169) in serious cases.

In matters relating to surnames (noms patronymiques), the Office of the Attorney General examines the applications for changes of name, including those concerning persons having recently acquired or recovered French nationality and wishing to have a French-sounding surname or name.

These functions are closely related to the supervision exercised by the Office of the Attorney General over the officers responsible for making entries in the civil status registers.

Within the framework of its supervisory role, the Office of the Attorney General acts as adviser to the officers in charge of the civil status registers in municipalities (communes) situated with the jurisdiction of the Regional Court.

In the commercial and economic sphere, the Office of the Attorney General has a supervisory role in relation to bankruptcies and, as already mentioned, in relation to the settlement of businesses' and traders' liabilities. It also ensures the enforcement of rules and regulations governing the banking professions, those relating to patents (law of 2 January 1968) and the licensing of premises where alcoholic beverages are consumed.

The Office of the Attorney General supervises the keeping of the commercial registers by the Principal Registrar of the Commercial Court.

With regard to voluntary organisations, the Office of the Attorney General has the power to take an organisation to the Regional Court, in order to have it wound up, if it is not properly constituted (Article 3 et seq. of the law of 1 July 1901).

The Office of the Attorney General has the same powers with regard to a trade union: it may apply for a trade union to be wound up if it is not constituted in accordance with legal requirements (Article L 461-1 of the Labour Code).

In relation to the press, the Office of the Attorney General receives notifications of the establishment of new newspapers and checks that the legal requirements have been met (Articles 7 and 10 of the law of 29 July 1881). It also supervises the legal filing of copies of publications (dépôt légal).

The Public Health Code requires the Attorney General to make regular visits to private and public institutions providing accommodation for persons of unsound mind, thus enabling such persons to make an official complaint directly to the representative of the Office of the Attorney General.

With regard to <u>education</u> the Office of the Attorney General has a duty to ensure that legislation concerning private education (enseignement libre) is complied with, as well as that concerning health and safety in the buildings where such education takes place. It also has a duty to check the qualifications and good character of teachers.

In these various areas of public life, civil liberties are at stake and through its supervision, the Office of the Attorney General ensures that they are respected.

## CONCLUSION

As we have seen, the Office of the Attorney General has a function which is at the heart of our democratic institutions, watching over the proper balance between the general interest and the interests of individuals, either through its protective action or through its supervision.

We have already noted that, among its judicial functions, it has a very important role as principal party in civil proceedings. Although traditionally, as stipulated in Article 1 of the New Code of Civil Procedure, which provides as follows:

"Only the parties may commence proceedings, except where the law provides otherwise",

the Office of the Attorney General acts as a joined party in civil proceedings, the legislator has increased the number of cases in which it may act proprio motu.

Based on the need to protect public policy, the law has given the Office of the Attorney General wide scope for intervention - to such an extent that it would appear this evolution has led to a shift of balance to the detriment of the interest of individuals.

But this would be too hasty a conclusion. Proof of the contrary can be found in an area which traditionally has been supervised by the Office of the Attorney General with the aim of protecting the general interest: that of civil status registration (état civil). Indeed, in this area, the Office of the Attorney General has moved towards recognition of the wishes of individuals.

We refer here to the Office of the Attorney General's response to requests by transsexuals for amendments to the civil status register. This response has evolved in accordance with our changes in our positive law.

In a judgment of 21 May 1990, despite a favourable medical report, the first civil division of the Court of Cassation refused to recognise transsexualism a true change of sex which would in turn justify a modification of civil status.

This judgment therefore rejected some of the implications of Article 8 (1) of the European Convention on Human Rights which says:

"Everyone has the right to respect for his private and family life'.

The Court of Cassation stressed that this text did not warrant "granting transsexuals a sex which is not theirs by birth.

In line with the position adopted by the European Commission of Human Rights in the 1980s, the European Court of Human Rights found France guilty of a violation on 25 March 1992, holding that the attitude of the French authorities to transsexuals constituted a violation of the respect for private and family life guaranteed by Article 8 of the European Convention on Human Rights.

The European Court based its decision on the following arguments:

"The applicant finds herself daily in a situation which, taken as a whole, is not compatible with the respect due to her private life" (...) "The applicant, as a result of the frequent necessity to disclose information concerning her private life to third parties, suffered distress which was too serious to be justified on the ground of respect for the rights of others."

The Court therefore ruled that "**the fair balance which has to be struck between the general interest and the interests of the individual has not been attained, and there has thus been a violation of Article 8 of the European Convention for the Protection of Human Rights**".

This message has finally been heard, and in a judgment delivered on 11 December 1992, the Court of Cassation, sitting in plenary, ruled that:

"Subject to compliance with certain medical conditions, transsexuals now have the right to obtain a change of name on the civil status register".

This ruling takes into account both the right to respect for private and family life (in Article 8 of the European Convention for the Protection of Human Rights) and the principle of inalienability of the status of individuals.

Consequently, in an area where the general interest is particularly at stake, the Office of the Attorney General now relies on the changes in positive law in order to perform a supervisory role which is favourable to the individual.

The Office of the Attorney General, by respecting the law and its institutions, and through its constant diligence in ensuring respect for the law and its institutions, acts as the instrument regulating the proper balance between the general interest and the wishes of individuals, such balance being necessary to the good functioning of a democracy.

To conclude, it is apposite to recall the principle contained in Article 8 (2) of the European Convention for the Protection of Human Rights.

"There shall be no interference by a public authority with the exercise of this right except such as is in accordance with the law and is necessary in a democratic society in the interests of national security, public safety or the economic well-being of the country, for the prevention of disorder or crime, for the protection of health and morals, or for the protection of the rights and freedoms of others."

The work of the Office of the Attorney General in the civil domain has to be seen in this light.

## TOPIC 5

## FUNCTIONS OF THE PUBLIC PROSECUTOR'S OFFICE IN CONNECTION WITH CIVIL LITIGATIONS AND ITS EXTRA JUDICIAL FUNCTIONS

**Nóra Katalin BONOMI**
Prosecutor
Prosecutor General's Office (Hungary)

### General Presentation of the solutions of Central and Eastern European countries

Based on answers from the different countries it can be established that prosecutories have their special place in the system of institutions created to protect legality in most of the Central and Eastern European countries. Although the role of prosecutories has been changed, and the authorization of prosecutors has been modified recently, activities of prosecutories in the field of protecting legality and observing the law are still considered important.

Activities of institutions which are created to protect legality are those of state institutions which are regulated by the law, aiming assertion of legality of decisions and procedures of state or local authorities as well as public officials, organizations and associations. This activity includes both ordinary and extraordinary legal remedies.

For all of the countries answering our questionnaire it can be generally established the final stage of protection of legality is the judicial proceedings or process of Constitutional Court.

The prosecutories are taking part in activities of organization dealing with protection or legality either with its own authority or assisting the process. The scope of authority of public prosecutors limited; but having wide range of power to investigate violations of law and initiate abandonment of unlawful action. Accordingly the public prosecutor accomplishing his task controls other organizations' decisions, and takes measures against harming the law.

In functions, related to civil litigation and general legality control there are plenty of similarities in Central and Eastern European countries Prosecutories, but there are also special solutions as will be shown.

In Albania and Republic of Belarus the prosecutors have the right to institute civil litigation if the person concerned is not able to defend his rights. Bulgaria has a similar solution as follows:

The prosecutor may lay actions to defend the rights and lawful interest of the citizens unless they are not "intiuitu personem" rights. The prosecutor can take part in a civil case by:

- laying an action
- entering civil procedures initiated by others
- giving conclusive statements about civil cases
- appealing the court's decisions.

The prosecutor may initiate all types of procedures provided for by Code of Civil Procedure.

In Hungary prosecutor had general authorization earlier, but the Constitutional Court has limited these rights by its decision in January 1/1994 (I.7). This decision maintain those statements of Code of Civil Procedure according to what a prosecutor has the right to initiate only in case when the party is not able to represent himself; the prosecutor hasn't the right to file an action for persons or organization specified in law. Beside of this Hungarian Prosecutory can initiate a process to protect and represent public interest only in cases specified by the law. There is more than fifty of different acts and regulations which authorize the prosecutor to institute judicial or extra-judicial processes.

The prosecutor has the right to file action in the following cases:

based on the act about the marriage, family and guardianship:
- determination of invalidity of marriage
- denial of paternity
- dissolution of adoption
- placement of a child
- abatement of parental right of supervision

based on Code of Civil Procedure
- arbitration

based on Civil Code
- abatement of foundation
- reverence laws
- bringing an action to repeal contract concluded by taking advantages of other party weakness
- placing charge of a guardian
- dissolution of a political party
- cancellation of an entry in the land register
- discrepancy in issue of bonds

The prosecutor can initiate an extrajudicial process
- prohibition of press items
- cancellation of an entry in register of firms

- protecting the right of invention
- to protect registered trade mark.

In Macedonia the public prosecutor is not entitled to institute litigation in cases, when the person interested is not able to defend his rights. The guardianship officials have that right.

In Poland the prosecutor has the right to initiate every civil litigation and also to take part in any civil proceedings being in course if according to his point of view there is necessity to guard law-abiding, civil rights or public interest. In matters concerning family the prosecutor may bring in complaint only in cases provided in law (Art. 7 of Code of Civil Procedure).

The prosecutor is obliged to take part in proceedings concerning acknowledgment of foreign judgment and interdiction of legal ability. Prosecutor may initiate legal civil proceedings in matters in which there is necessity to bring back the state of law accordance by court judgment if appropriate subjects restrain from institution of such proceedings or they are incapable to act. Generally this kind of prosecutorial activity concerns damages and personal harms as a consequence of an offence.

Prosecutor may also bring a complaint against defendant until the time of institution the trial phase. This document containing demand of compensation for harm or damages is carried together with the file of indictment to the court.

In Russia in accordance with Art. 31 of Act on Prosecutory the public prosecutor has the right to initiate action to protect the rights or interest of a person. A similar solution is given in the Code of Civil Proceedings.

The Chief Public Prosecutor in his Directive of 28.05.1992 instructed the prosecutors to use their rights mainly to protect interest which is not evident obvious or not related to a person.

In the practice of the Romanian prosecutor there is the civil litigation to deal with.

In Slovakia only in expressly stipulated cases has the prosecutor the right to institute civil litigation:

- determination of invalidity of a contract about the sale of state property,
- denial of paternity,
- determination whether a strike is lawful or not,
- dissolution of a political party (political movement),
- judicial review of administrative acts from the view-point of their legality - if the prosecutor's protest was not met by the administrative authority.

In other cases prosecutor hasn't the right to institute civil litigation, even the person concerned is not able to defend his/her rights.

The prosecutor is not entitled to institute litigation in this cases. The guardianship officials have that right.

In Slovenia a public prosecutor may not appeal in civil proceedings on behalf of a party who is not legally capable. According to the law on legal proceedings, a party who is not legally capable is represented by legal advocate, which is determined by law or act which is issued by a competent state body on the basis of law. In a non-legal proceeding, which mainly arrange relations between affected person who are parties to the proceeding, the law on non-legal proceedings determines that some proceedings in which there is an expressed public interest shall be commenced on the proposal of a public prosecutor. These proceedings are:

- a proceeding for taking over parental rights
- a proceeding for taking over business capacity
- a proceeding for declaring a missing person dead
- a proceeding for proving death.

Besides the right to initiate an action the prosecutor has the power to intervene in any phase of litigation going on. However there are some alterations or limitations in different countries.

In Albania the prosecutors do not any longer have the power to intervene with civil proceedings between private parties. They can participate in civil proceedings when there is evidence of existence of the public or state interest is involved.

In Republic of Belarus and in Bulgaria the prosecutors have the above mentioned rights, in addition in Bulgaria under the Art. 27 par. 2 of the Code of Civil Procedure the prosecutor may give conclusive statements in civil cases when it is provided by the law or when he find it is necessary.

In Hungary the above mentioned decision of the Constitutional Court has abandoned the right of prosecutors to intervene in any stage of the litigation.

In Poland the prosecutor has the power to intervene.

In Romania only in the cases stipulated by law strictly personal civil litigations.

In Russia in some cases when it is defined by the law the prosecutor is obliged to take part in the litigation. Such cases are for instance

- restitution of employment
- ejectment without providing any other place for living
- action of citizen in case the press is harming his reputation on honour
- in actions which were initiated by the prosecutor.

The prosecutor and his deputy have the right to appeal to higher court in all cases when they consider that the decision of the court is unlawful.

In Slovakia the prosecutor still have the power to intervene in civil litigation (he may enter civil proceeding) only in expressly stipulated cases regarding:

- individuals capacity to legal acts,
- declaration that the missing person is dead,
- entry of a company in the Corporate Register (Commercial Register),
- the upbringing of minors,
- guardianship.

In these cases the Prosecutor General may file a complaint against violation of the law to contest a final decision of a court.

In other cases prosecutor has not the right to intervene in civil litigations.

In Slovenia the law on legal proceedings envisages the participation of a public prosecutor in litigation, which is taking place between other persons if the suspicion exist that one or both parties are using their right in the proceeding such that they would prevent the use of mandatory regulations on administering or disposing of social resources, or that they would evade financial obligations to the community or would prevent the use of mandatory provisions of international contracts. In such a case, a public prosecutor has the right to propose within the limitations of the plaintiff's demands, that they establish also facts which the parties have not mentioned and evidence which the parties have not submitted, and the right to use legal means.

The prosecutor's functions of general legality control can be observed in a limited number of countries, because this functions have been abandoned in Albania, Macedonia, Poland and Romania.

In Slovakia according to the Act concerning prosecutors, the scope of the general supervisory control extends to the executive, local authorities and to all legal persons. In reality, the general supervisory control over the legal persons is not performed. The most significant change in this field was the abolishing of prosecutors supervision over the legality of procedure and decisions of court.

The general supervisory power has been remodelled through an orientation on the protection of individual rights and public interest.

The general legality control of Bulgaria, Russia and in Hungary shows a lot of similar features. There competence is of approximately the same scope.

In Bulgaria it mainly concerns ministries, local administration, officials and the citizens.

In Russia it is a little wider because the controlling other regulating or controlling institutions, enterprises, authorities, military bodies, social or political movements or organizations, or legal personalities, including legality of the decisions made by them, according to the Act of Prosecutory dated 17.01.1992.

However in Bulgaria after designing the new judiciary the scope of the general supervision shall be seriously limited since the Administrative Court is to be established. A three-instance trial and cassation shall also be introduced.

The Hungarian Act of prosecutors defines in a mostly similar way the circle of competence of general legality control:

- It involves decisions regarding individual and normative measures made by administrative organizations lower than governmental level.

- It also concerns decisions settling disputes out of the court as well as state and cooperative employment.

This controlling tasks involve stating whether these normatives and decisions are in harmony with the stipulations of the Constitution and acts.

The Hungarian prosecutories are not entitled to observe practicability, economy and deliberation of authorities and organizations.

In the case of non-compliance the prosecutor is supposed to make legal step on the protection of legality. He can warn the leaders of the concerned organization. The strongest means of administrative law supervision is to protest on legal ground against an unlawful decision. The public prosecutor's office could propose in his paper the suspending of the execution too. If the organization does not agree with the protest it has to pass it to its superior organization. If they do not accept the measure the prosecutor can initiate an action.

The judicial review does not exclude the general legality control because one cannot expect a client to oppose or to file an action against a favourable decision even if it is unlawful, still in order to protect public interest there must be means of legal remedy. That is the reason why the general legality control has justification besides judicial review.

In Russia the general supervisory control has further developed.

Regarding the present historical situation taking into consideration demands of building of the state and the interest of development of the society the subject of the general supervisory control is not only the law or the acts itself, but also the implementation of the presidential resolution concerning general regulations.

Because of the recent changes in the field of political, social and economic life it is necessary to make stronger the protecting activity of the prosecutories. Now the protection of the rights of the citizens, their freedom and their legal interest are prevailing.

Protection of starting companies has became a new part of the tasks of the prosecutory. Of course the tasks of protecting the economic interest of the state remain important.

The general supervisory power exists even as an aspect of the conception of the judicature reform. Before it is changed, the functions in protection legality, which were practiced by the prosecutory, cannot be overtaken by the courts. The prosecutor has the right to turn to the court for final solution if their first steps didn't bring success.

In Slovenia the characteristics of the general supervisory control are as follows:

The function of public prosecutor includes the protection of legality relates equally to concrete decisions issued in civil, non legal and criminal proceedings and administrative proceedings if such is defined by law as well as in regulations and general acts issued for exercising public authority, if a question is raised of the constitutionality and legality of regulations or act in connection with proceedings which are conducted by a prosecutor.

A prosecutor has even the right to demand the annulment or suspension of implementation of a legally enforceable judgment or administrative decision if he ascertains that there are grounds for the use of legal means against such a decision because of a violation of the Constitution, law or international contract.

An important innovation in this field is contained in the new law on the Constitutional Court which took effect on 2.4.1994, and which involved harmonization with the provisions of the Constitution of Republic of Slovenia.

The Constitutional Court is the highest body of judicial authority for the protection of constitutionality and legality and human rights and basic freedoms, and according to the new legislation, it has the right in proceeding for assessing constitutionality and legality of regulations and general acts issued for exercise of public authority in whole or in part to annul a law which is not in accordance with the Constitution.

The Constitutional Court may annul anticonstitutional and illegal regulations or general acts issued for the exercise of public authority.

The law on the Constitutional Court defines in addition to the state prosecutor also: the National Assembly, a third of the delegates to the National Assembly, the Council of State, the Government, the courts, the Bank of Slovenia, the accountancy court, the Ombudsman, representative bodies of local communities and representative trade unions for the region of the state. An initiative for commencing a proceeding may also be given by anyone who demonstrates a legal interest.

Let us finish the short summary of the answers sent by ten Central and Eastern European countries' prosecutories regarding the civil litigation and general supervisory control.

Although - as one can see - the solutions for these tasks are different in different countries, but from point of view of protection of legality, similar discussions and studies are considered useful means to make our knowledge wider, to give all of us new ideas in solving the problem of renewal of our legal system.

# TOPIC 5

# FUNCTIONS OF THE PUBLIC PROSECUTOR'S OFFICE IN CONNECTION WITH CIVIL LITIGATIONS AND ITS EXTRA JUDICIAL ACTIVITY

**Jerzy SZYMANSKI**
**Prosecutor (Poland)**

However some of the functions of the prosecutor's office in Republic of Poland have been limited in 1990, the prosecutorial activity in connection with civil litigations and extra judicial functions are still important and socially useful.

Out of necessity, this can only be a brief summary of principles, legislation and regulations dealing with the problem. Therefore only the most important institutions concerned should be described in general.

If the audience has an opportunity to get to know some of the extra - penal functions of the public prosecutor in the Republic of Poland, the task of this paper will be accomplished.

I. **The participation of the prosecutor in civil litigation.**

The institution of prosecutorial activity in civil litigations has been known in numerous countries for many years. The first country to bring this procedure into legal system was France - by decree from 1810. Italy and Germany brought it in use in the 30s and 40s of XX century. In Poland before the second World War the institution was known but the participation of the prosecutor in civil litigations was rather inconspicuous. In the general change of Polish civil procedure performed in 1950 the institution of participation of the prosecutor in civil cases as an independent subject of civil procedure has been regulated and increased. The practice of applying this institution was adapted to purposes and needs of the system of that time. The participation of the prosecutor in many civil cases had political character as well.

Later legal grounds of prosecutorial participation in civil litigations have been described in art. 7 of the Code of Civil Procedure issued in 1965. Regulations with some changes in this field have been in force until now. Art. 7 states:
"The prosecutor is authorized to require the instituting of every civil litigation and also to participate in any civil proceedings being in course if according to his point of view there is a necessity to protect law-abidingness, civil rights or social interest. In family cases not involving property the prosecutor may bring the claim only in cases defined in legal provisions". However the provision mentioned above concerns only two forms of participation in this proceeding i.e. demand or instituting of the civil litigation and

accession to the case being in course, art. 7 of the Code of Civil Procedure contains general direction describing the grounds of all prosecutorial actions including the means of appeals, objection to a judgement by default, petition for the revival of proceedings.

The statement: "the prosecutor may demand to institute a civil proceedings" indicates also the possibility to apply every form of instituting legal proceedings, for example by lodging means of appeal.

It is worth mentioning that the legislator has placed art. 7 in a general part of the Code of Civil Procedure containing the most important principles of procedure.

The Law of the Public Prosecutor's Office from 20 March 1985 in wording of an Act established by Law from 15 May 1993 stated that one of the main tasks of the Public Prosecution Office - protecting law-abidingness (besides looking after the prosecution of crimes) is carried out by the Prosecutor General and subordinated to him public prosecutors who institute actions in criminal proceedings (adhesion claims) and civil procedure, participate in civil proceedings and in cases concerning employees rights and social insurance if according to prosecutor's appreciation there is a necessity to protect legality, social interest, social property or civil rights.

According to the established juristic doctrines the public prosecutor was created by the provision of art.7 of the above mentioned Code and these regulations of statutes concerning special matters i.e. Family and Guardianship Code supplying the prosecutor with the right of bringing actions in defined categories of cases.

There are many opinions in Polish doctrine related to the position of the prosecutor in civil litigations i.e. whether the public prosecutor should be named as a party of the case or otherwise. The prevailing views are that the prosecutor in Civil litigations is the independent party in a situation when he has brought an action in the public interest, not in favour of a certain person, but against all persons concerned being parties of a legal relation. If the prosecutor institutes an action in favour of the person concerned he is not recognized as a party in civil proceedings because he has no right to dispose the subject matter of a lawsuit (art. 56 & 2 of Code of Civil Procedure).

The prosecutor is recognized as a party in civil proceedings in family cases not involving property. If the prosecutor is taking the role of a party in a litigation being in course instituted by another claimant, by the terms of art. 60 of the Code of Civil Procedure he is not dependent to any party of the case. In this situation the prosecutor is an independent party of the proceedings having capacity to declare statements, motions and bring facts and evidences.

The act of taking the place of a party by the prosecutor in civil litigations instituted by the person concerned is not under control of the court. It is the independent right of the prosecutor. By the terms of art. 59 of the Law of Civil Procedure the court is obliged to inform the prosecutor about the case in which his participation is desirable. The court is also obligated to serve the prosecutor a judgement by default (art. 343). The prosecutor is authorized to estimate if his participation in certain proceeding is in fact desirable or not. When the action is brought by the prosecutor in favour of the person involved, the court is obligated to inform this person by serving the copy of the statement of claim. In this case the person concerned may take the place of a plaintiff in any stage of the proceeding (art. 56). In cases instituted by the prosecutor the judgement of the court possesses validity in law (res iudicata) between the person in favour of whose the prosecutor has brought an action and the respondent. But the valid judgements in cases concerning property do not deprive the person concerned, who has not participated in the proceeding the right to claim entirely or partly (art. 58). In family cases not involving property the prosecutor may bring an action only in matters provided for by the law.

By the terms of the Family and Guardianship Code the public prosecutor is authorized to bring an action before the court demanding: nullification of a marriage, establishment of the existence or non - existence of a marriage (art. 22), establishment or denial of the parentage of a child or nullification of the fathering a child born out of wedlock (art.86), dissolution of adoption (art. 127). In cases relating to family the prosecutor has no right to file a statement of claim concerning divorce.

The public prosecutor may also institute other kinds of proceedings e.g. non-litigious proceedings, executive proceedings.

Actually binding Regulations in Public Prosecution Office have established some practical rules governing the prosecutor's activity in this field, e.g. the prosecutor must not participate in cases before the court when the parties have a good civil law protection or when the interest of the State Treasury is well represented by the organizational unit concerned. Before bringing action in favour of a certain individual before propounding motion for conservation of claim it is desirable when the prosecutor communicates with the person concerned informing him about his rights and obligations. Sometimes it happens that the person does not intend to vindicate a claim. In such a situation the prosecutor must not act. Action based on art. 412 of Civil Code (in wording of an Act from 28 July 1990) is brought by the prosecutor frequently while conducting criminal proceedings relating to unlawful acceptance of profit by public functionary or alluding to influential acquaintance (bribery, paid patronage). This provision states: "The court may decide the forfeiture to the benefit of fiscus the object of performance if the latter has been consciously completed in return for the commission of an illegal or wicked act. If the object of performance has been wasted the court may decide the forfeiture of equivalence in cash". simplifying, the prosecutor may bring an action to the court against the person validly sentenced e.g. for bribery demanding in civil proceeding adjudication forfeiture of a thing or equivalence in cash deriving from an offense. If the public prosecutor does not file a statement of a claim based on this provision he is obliged to inform an organ responsible for vindication in favour of the State Treasure (Financial Office). Judicial decision inflicting forfeiture of money of assets deriving from an illegal act (or wicked act) is based on facultative provision of art. 412 of the Civil Code (in wording of an Act from 28 July 1990). Till that time the aforesaid provision had contained the rule of obligatory forfeiture.

In some categories of civil cases the participation of the prosecutor is obligatory. These cases concern legal incapacitation and the recognition of a foreign court decision.

In cases concerning claims ensuing from property rights the prosecutor before bringing an action ought to demand in writing the fulfilment of an obligation. In practice the fulfilment of an obligation on the demand of the prosecutor occurs frequently and because of that the instituting legal proceeding is not needed.

According to the accepted in the Polish Prosecution Office practice the most desirable prosecutor's claims are in cases concerning:

- damages caused by the public functionaries while performing duties,
- exemption from execution assets seized in the course of criminal proceedings,
- protection of the family,
- protection of the natural environment,
- damages and injuries caused by perpetrators of acts of hooligan nature.

The prosecutor's participation in proceedings concerning matters of family and guardianship nature is particularly needed in cases relating to:

- taking away a child,
- denial of paternity or nullification (annulment) of fathering a child born out of wedlock,
- adoption of a child by a foreigner,
- annulment or establishment of the existence or non-existence of a marriage.

In cases respecting claims under a contract of employment and related to social insurance the prosecutor ought to act in situations when:

- the employee's interest has been jeopardized by a rank breach of law,
- the injured employee is not able to act by his single-handed efforts (helplessness),
- as a result of negligence of the employer the injured employee has not obtained adequate compensation.

If according to the prosecutor's estimation a valid judicial decision is in contradiction with the law or the interest of the Republic of Poland, the prosecutor ought to submit a proper motion with files to the Prosecutor General containing a request of an extraordinary appeal against a final sentence.

## II. Public prosecutor's activity in the administrative law domain.

After the amending of the Law of the Public Prosecution Office from 22 March 1990 introducing changes in the prosecutor's activity, prosecutorial tasks in extra-judicial field have been restricted to participation in administrative proceedings or other procedures in which the participation of the prosecutor is provided by special regulations. It especially concerns cases in which a violation of the law or the inactivity of certain organs aim at the interest of the Republic of Poland. The public prosecutor has in his disposal the legal means provided by the provisions of the Code of Administrative Procedure, the Law of the Public Prosecution Office and special regulation in the form of:

- a motion for instituting administrative proceedings in the purpose of eliminate the state of contradiction with the law (art. 82 of adore-said Code),

- a declaration of participation in a proceeding being in course from the prosecutor's initiative or at the suggestion of a certain organ (but the participation in proceeding depends on the prosecutor-art. 183 of the Code),

- means of appeal in the course of the administrative proceedings (art.188),

- objections against final decisions (art.184),

- a motion to the local government or regional state authorities (voivode) containing a request concerning changing or abating the act being in contradiction with the law (art.5 of the Law of the Public Prosecution Office),

- motions containing a request concerning the abating of the resolutions issued by the organs of local government moved to organs of supervision,

- claims to the administrative court against administrative decisions being in contradiction with the law concerning e.g.: architecture, architecture supervision, town-planning, prizes, duties, public roads, geology, communal administration, employment, agriculture, forestry, health service, etc.

According to the established practice the public prosecutor has the right to use ordinary means of appeal. He refuses to undertake action at the demand of a party if the administrative proceedings have not been finished, and the party may independently vindicate it's rights and the rights and the refusal is not in contradiction with the interest of the Republic of Poland. The party has in disposal means of appeal or a claim to an administrative court. Some acts in the mentioned procedure may be undertaken only by the supreme prosecution organ. In such a case a competent public prosecutor presents files of the case to the Prosecutor General together with the deposed motions. This action takes place when there is a necessity of:

- lodging an extraordinary appeal against a final sentence issued by an administrative court,

- moving an objection against the administrative decision issued by the supreme or central organ of state administration,

- intervention to the supreme or central organ of the state administration, which has issued a normative act, containing request of the abatement or nullification of it before moving to the Constitutional Tribunal with a motion for the approval of legality of this act, i.e. accordance with the Constitution (art. 5 of the Law of the Public Prosecution Office),

- Intervention to the Constitutional Tribunal for the establishment of a commonly binding interpretation of the law. (art. 4 of the adore-said Law),

- a motion to the Prime Minister for the abatement of the order (regulation) issued by the voivodeship administration.

The district prosecutor may propound-through the channel of the Division of Public Prosecution in Ministry of Justice - objections against decisions issued by the central state administrative courts. The efficiency of these means is very high. It is worth while to say that the former provisions authorized public prosecutor to deal with supervisory control (the prosecutor's control of law-abidingness) have been repealed by the Law of the Public Prosecution Office form 22 March 1990. So actually, the prosecutor in Poland is not authorised up to take up control concerning certain problems or matters from the view-point of legality. But the prosecutor may and ought to take up actions and move means provided by the provisions of Code of Administrative Procedure in certain adore-said individual cases.

The task of protecting law - abidingness the prosecutor may fulfil also by notifying the organs of the local government about his observations concerning contraventions of law which have been disclosed during performing the prosecutor's official duties. The grounds for such notifications are provided in the provision of art. 2 and 3 of the Law of the Public Prosecution Office.

# CONCLUSIONS AND RECOMMENDATIONS

## TOPIC 1

**Conclusions**

Political changes and constitutional reforms in the region had different impacts on the constitutional position of the "Prokuratura" during the past few years.

The countries whose prosecutorial system has been analysed can be divided into three groups:

The first group is of those that maintained the independent constitutional position of the Public Prosecution office in its form inherited from the old regime (six countries). In these countries the Public Prosecution Office is independent from the Executive and connected only to the Legislative.

The second group consists of those countries which created a new type of independence (three countries). In these countries the Public Prosecution Office became part of the Judiciary.

The third group comprises those countries where the Public Prosecution Office is subordinated to the Executive, namely to the Minister of Justice (two countries).

Certain classical basic principles prevail independently of the constitutional position. The most characteristic ones are as follows:

- the prosecution agencies are independent of the courts;
- the Public prosecution Office is a centralised and vertically organised institution;
- it is hierarchically structured and a line of command exists within the organisation;
- the prosecution agencies are organised with respect to the court system and the administrative structure of the country.

The constitutional position and the scope of functions of the prosecutorial organisation of individual countries may be different, but the determinative circumstance is that it operates in a democratic society.

*Recommendations*

1. Since the Public Prosecution Office plays a fundamental role in the administration of justice and in some countries it also has extra-judicial and

other functions in maintaining the observance of law, the position of the chief of the prosecutorial organisation as well as the character of its relationships with other institutions, authorities and agencies (Parliament, Executive, Judiciary) should be precisely defined in the Constitution and the law with respect of the rule of law as well as the demands of functional autonomy.

2. It is advisable that any political decision on the constitutional position of the Public Prosecution Office takes into consideration the democratic legal traditions of the country. The decision should bring about a solution that preserves the confidence of the public.

3. Governing principles of organisational subordination of either the Public Prosecution office to other State organs, or individual prosecutors to internal or external superiors should take into account that prosecutors to internal or external superiors should take into account that prosecutors should be subject only to the law and, therefore, free from illegal influence, and should ensure the protection of human rights without discrimination.

## TOPIC 2

**Conclusions**

The elaborated regulation of the status of prosecutors existing in many western systems provides examples to the East and Central European countries, as far as they are in accord with their own culture and traditions, since there is no ideal model. These countries have already made some progress in this field.

One of the new developments in the region is that those countries where the Public Prosecution Office is independent by being part of the Judiciary have created a new organ: a High Council of the Judiciary. There are different constitutional techniques by which political neutrality or political well-balancing of this body may be assured. The High Council of the Judiciary has competence, to a different extent, in cases related to the status of prosecutors.

In most countries of the region there is no systematic evaluation and promotion system. in some countries judicial control is already provided against decisions taken in disciplinary cases of prosecutors. Most of the countries seem to be in a real transitional period where the old system has already been abandoned and a new one has not been established yet.

*Recommendations*

4. It is absolutely necessary to distinguish between the organisational (i.e. constitutional) position of the Public Prosecution Office and that of the functional autonomy prosecutors should enjoy when exercising their functions.

5.  Provisions relating to the status of prosecutors should provide necessary and objective guarantees to ensure the functional autonomy of individual prosecutors by determining:

    *   their career (appointment, high level professional training and promotion);
    *   their evaluation (transparency);
    *   the disciplinary proceedings and punishments.

6.  It would be beneficial to take inspiration from experiences of other countries or to find new solutions or improve the methods applied.

## TOPIC 3

**Conclusions**

The tasks and powers of the Central and Eastern European prosecution services in the field of criminal proceedings used to be similar to those of their Western counterparts with continental-type criminal procedural systems. The main differences were in human rights-matters: the prosecutor was entitled either to decide, or to sanction or approve others' decisions in matters concerning fundamental human rights like search, seizure and preliminary confinement-warrants.

The legislative changes that have already appeared or are envisaged in this respect are in line with the demands expressed by international instruments on human rights: they serve the implementation of judicial control in the phase of preliminary proceedings when human rights are concerned and to create a better balance between prosecution and defence by widening the rights of the defence or/and limiting the powers of the prosecutor.

*Recommendations*

7.  Initiatives aimed at the implementation of judicial control in preliminary proceedings when human rights are concerned and to achieve a just balance between prosecution and the defence are to be encouraged. On the other hand, the necessity and possibility of introduction or extension of prosecutors' discretionary powers with due respect to the national traditions of the system and international standards should be considered.

# TOPIC 4

**Conclusions**

In almost all countries, prosecutors play a crucial role in mutual assistance in criminal matters and in transfer of proceedings, while their role in extradition cases is in most countries an auxiliary one.

The prosecutorial functions connected to international co-operation are as a general rule centralised, but there is a growing tendency to decentralise, especially in countries which have traditional and intensive bilateral relations.

The way of transmission of letters rogatory depends on the character and the importance of the individual case; in neither country is the diplomatic channel the exclusive way.

Police in neither country have an autonomous role in mutual assistance, they can neither request nor grant legal assistance within their own competence.

The lack of knowledge of the legal provisions, the language and the competent prosecutors of the other countries represents the most characteristic problems in international co-operation.

*Recommendations*

8.  In order to master the challenges that all states are confronted with as a result of the opening of the borders and the rise in transboundary crime, a far-reaching co-operation in criminal matters, including co-operation between prosecution offices, should be further promoted. The close-knit network of Council of Europe conventions in the penal field should to the widest extend possible be made the instrument for co-operation between prosecutors in Europe.

9.  To that end, the competencies and responsibilities of prosecutors in national criminal proceedings and in international co-operation should be regulated in a manner that meets generally recognised standards in the field of criminal law and in the protection of human rights and fundamental freedoms.

10. The separation of the tasks and responsibilities of prosecutors form those of the police should for the purpose of ensuring judicial control over police intervention and should be regulated and practised in a way that excludes incompatibilities with differing models in other states.

# TOPIC 5

**Conclusions**

The role of the prosecutors relating to civil litigation and extra-judicial functions has changed in almost all countries to a diverging extent.

The extent and the quality of the changes depend on the sort of new institutions that have already started to work.

*Recommendations*

11. The intervention in civil litigation by the Public Prosecution Office should be for the purpose of the protection of public and justified private interest by the state, as prescribed by law.

12. The remaining elements of the former "supervisory control" should be directed towards the protection of the democratic legality, rule of law, human rights, fundamental freedoms and the public interest.

# PROGRAMME

**Monday, 26 September** Arrival of participants

**Tuesday, 27 September**

    Opening session

        Chair: **Imre KERTÉSZ**, Professor Adviser at the Prosecutor General's Office

09h 00 Addresses of welcome

    **Árpád GÖNCZ**
    President of the Republic of Hungary

    **Pál VASTAGH**
    Minister of Justice of the Republic of Hungary

    **Marie-Odile WIEDERKEHR**
    Deputy Director of Legal Affairs, Council of Europe

    **Kálmán GYÖRGYI**
    Prosecutor General of the Republic of Hungary

09h 30 Break

09h 40 Proposal and decision on the chairperson of each working section and on the procedure of drafting and passing conclusions and recommendations

10h 00 Break

10h 30 Introductory Lecture: The Public Prosecutor's Office in the transitional period

    **Kálmán GYÖRGYI**
    Prosecutor General of the Republic of Hungary

11h 10 Break

11h 15   Press Conference (the ground floor hall of the Hotel Hadik)

11h 45   Lunch

13h 30   First Working Session

> Chair:   **S. KEKLEROV**, Prosecutor General of the Russian Federation

Topic 1:   **The constitutional status and the internal structure of the Public Prosecution in a State governed by the rule of law**

* Presentation of synthesis and national reports
* followed by general discussion

Rapporteurs:

**José Manuel SANTOS PAIS**
Attorney General's Office (Portugal)

Presentation of Topic 1 in its Pan-European context

**Attila HLAVATHY**
Director, Prosecutor General's Office (Hungary)

General Presentation of the solutions of Central and Eastern European countries

15h 30   Break

16h 00   Second Working Session

> Chair: **V. STURZA**, Minister of Justice, Moldova

Topic 2:   **Selection and status of prosecutors and the management of the prosecutor's office**

* Presentation of synthesis and national reports
* followed by general discussion

Rapporteurs:

**François CORDIER**
Premier Substitut du Procureur de la République de Paris (France)

Presentation of Topic 2 in its Pan-European context

**Iiona LÉVAI**
Head of Division, Prosecutor General's Office (Hungary)

General presentation of the solutions of Central and Eastern European countries

19h 00    Reception given by the Prosecutor General of Hungary during a two hour pleasure boat trip on the Danube

**Wednesday, 28 September**

09h 00    Third Working Session

Chair:   S. ZIKOV, Deputy Prosecutor of The Former Yugoslav Republic of Macedonia

Topic 3:    **Prosecutorial functions in connection with criminal law: pre-trial functions; discretionary power; trial functions**

* Presentation of synthesis and national reports
* followed by general discussion

Rapporteurs:

**Birgitte VESTBERG**
Staatsadvokaten for Fyn (Denmark)

Presentation of Topic 3 in its Pan-European context

**Endre BÓCZ**
Prosecutor General of Budapest (Hungary)

General presentation of the solutions of Central and Eastern European countries

**Boyan Rangelov STANKOV**
Prosecutor, Deputy President of the Council for Criminological Researches at the Chief Prosecutor's Office (Bulgaria)

Presentation of the specific solution of Bulgaria

10h 30   Break

11h 00    Continuation of the general discussion

12h 00 Lunch

14h 00 Continuation of the general discussion

15h 00 Break

15h 30 Fourth Working Session

        Chair: S. LAIFER, Director of the International Section, Office of the Prosecutor, Slovakia

Topic 4: **The role of prosecutors in the application of international criminal law; mutual assistance in criminal matters, transfer of criminal proceedings, extradition, etc.**

    \* Presentation of synthesis and national reports
    \* followed by general discussion

Rapporteurs:

**Peter WILKITZKI**
Ministerialrat, Bundesministerium der Justiz (Germany)

Presentation of Topic 4 in its Pan-European context

**László LÁNG**
Director, Prosecutor General's Office (Hungary)

General presentation of the solutions of the countries of Central and Eastern Europe

19h 00 Hungarian-style dinner, at the invitation of Mr Zoltán GÁL, Speaker of the Parliament of the Republic of Hungary, at the Hotel Hadik

### Thursday, 29 September

09h 00  Fifth Working Session

        Chair:  **Dan APOSTOL**, Prosecutor at the Supreme Court of Romania

    Topic 5:    **Functions of the public prosecutor's office in connection with civil litigations and its extra judicial functions**

        * Presentation of synthesis and national reports
        * followed by general discussion

        Rapporteurs:

        **Christian PAUL-LOUBIÈRE**
        Magistrat au Tribunal de grande instance de Paris, Chargé des Travaux dirigés à l'Université de Paris Panthéon-Sorbonne (France)

        Presentation of Topic 5 in its Pan-European context

        **Nóra Katalin BONOMI**
        Prosecutor, Prosecutor General's Office (Hungary)

        General presentation of the solutions of the countries of Central and Eastern Europe

        **Jerzy SZYMANSKI**
        Prosecutor at the Prosecutor General's Office of Appeal in Gdansk (Poland)

        Presentation of the specific solution of Poland

10h 30  Break

11h 00  Closing Session

        Chair:  **Imre KERTÉSZ**
        Professor Adviser at the Prosecutor General's Office (Hungary)

        **Presentation and adoption of conclusions and recommendations**

        General Rapporteur:

        **Endre BÓCZ**

**Closing Speeches**

**Marie-Odile WIEDERKEHR**
Deputy Director of Legal Affairs, Council of Europe

**Kálmán GYÖRGYI**
Prosecutor General of the Republic of Hungary

13h 00 Lunch

14h 30 \* Presentation

made by the representative of the International Committee for the establishment of an International Association of Prosecutors

\* followed by general consultation

on

**the international co-operation of prosecutors**

for

\* all participants showing interest in the matter
\* personalities invited by the Commission

16h 00 Departure of participants

# LIST OF PARTICIPANTS / LISTE DES PARTICIPANTS

### ALBANIA / ALBANIE

Mr Alush DRAGOSHI, Prosecutor General of Albania, Prokuroria e Pergjithshme, TIRANA

Mr Edison HEBA, Public Prosecutor, Director of Legal Research and International Relations Department, Prokuroria e Pergjithshme, TIRANA, Albania

### BELARUS

Mr Oleg A SHABLUKO, Senior Assistant to the Procurator General of Belarus, Internationalnaya St. 22, MINSK 220050

Mr Semen V SKARULIS, Deputy of the Procurator of the Minsk Region of Belarus, Internationalnaya St. 22, MINSK 220050

### BULGARIA / BULGARIE

Mr Nestor NESTEROV, City Prosecutor of Sofia, City Prosecutor's Office, 2 Vitosha str, SOFIA 1000

### CROATIA / CROATIE

Mrs Bozica CVJETKO, Deputy Public Attorney of the Republic of Croatia, Avenija Vukovar 86, 41000 ZAGREB

Mr Ivan PLEVKO, Deputy District Attorney of Zagreb, Avenija Vukovar 86, 41000 ZAGREB

### CZECH REPUBLIC / REPUBLIQUE TCHEQUE

Mr Jiří BROŽ, Deputy Director, Legislative Department of the Ministry of Justice, Vyšehradská 16, 12810 PRAGUE 2

Mr Jaromir PATOČKA, Deputy Prosecutor General, Namesti Hrdinu 1300, Prague 4

### ESTONIA / ESTONIE

Mr Alar KIRS, Vice-Prosecutor General, State Prosecutor's Office, Wismari 7, EE - 0100 TALLINN

Mr Indrek MEELAK, Chief Public Prosecutor, State Prosecutor's Office, Wismari 7, EE - 0100 TALLINN

## LATVIA / LETTONIE

Mr Uldis DZENITIS, Deputy of the State Secretary, Ministry of Justice, Brivibas Bd 34, 1536 RIGA

Ms Regina EIZE, Head of the Department of Public Law, Ministry of Justice, Brivibas Bd 34, 1536 RIGA

## LITHUANIA / LITUANIE

Mr Sigitas JANKAUSKAS, Chief Prosecutor of the Unit of the Prosecutor General's office, A Smetones str 4, VILNIUS 2709

## FORMER YUGOSLAV REPUBLIC OF MACEDONIA / EX-RÉPUBLIQUE YOUGOSLAVE DE MACÉDOINE

Mr Vanko PAVLOSKI, Deputy Public Prosecutor of the Republic of Macedonia, Municipal Public Prosecutor's Office, Bul Krste Misirkov BB, Jauno Obuinitelstvo na, SKOPJE

Mr Sterjo ZIKOV, Deputy Public Prosecutor, Municipal Public Prosecutor's Office, Bul. Goce Delgev BB, Odstinsko Jauno Obuinitelstvo, SKOPJE,

## MOLDOVA

Mr Dumitru POSTOVAN, General Prosecutor of the Republic of Moldova, 26 str. Banulescu-Bodone, CHISINAU, 277012

Mr Vasile STURZA, Minister of Justice, Ministry of Justice, 73, bd Stefan cel Mare, CHISINAU, Moldova

## POLAND/POLOGNE

Mr Stanislav IWANICKI, Deputy Attorney General, ul Aleje Ujazdowrue 11 WARSAW

Mr Ryszard STEFANSKI, Head of Section, Ministry of Justice, ul st Kazury 2, d u 3 02795 WARSAW

## ROMANIA / ROUMANIE

Mr Dan APOSTOL, Prosecutor, General Prosecutor's Office, Boulevard Unirii 2 - 4, Sector 5, BUCAREST, Romania

Ms Rotaru PARASCHIVA, Prosecutor, Prosecutor's Office at the Apellate Court of Bucharest, BUCHAREST, Boulevard Unirii 2-4, secteur 5

**RUSSIAN FEDERATION / FEDERATION DE RUSSIE**

M. Sabir KEKHLEROV, Procureur Général-Adjoint de la Fédération de Russie

M. Gueorguï SMIRNOV, Directeur du Département du Ministère Public de Russie

**SLOVAK REPUBLIC / REPUBLIQUE SLOVAQUE**

Mr. Stanislav LAIFER, Prosecutor, Head of International Division, General Prosecutor's Office, Generalia Prosuraira Slovensky Republik, Zupné namestie 13, BRATISLAVA

Mr. Boris SPITZER, Prosecutor, Director of Non-penal section, General Prosecutor's Office of the Slovak Republic, Zupné namesti 13, 81285 BRATISLAVA

**SLOVENIA / SLOVENIE**

Apologies / Excusé

**UKRAINE**

Mr Alexander BONDARENKO, Procurator of the Zakarpatsky region, General Procurator's Office of Ukraine, 7 Dovzenko street, Uzhgorod, 294017 KIEV

Mr Oleg UMANSKY, Procurator of the International relations Department, 13/15 Riznitska street, 252011 KYIV

**RAPPORTEURS**

Mr Endre BÓCZ, Prosecutor General of Budapest, Markó u. 27, 1881 BUDAPEST, (Hungary)

M. François CORDIER, Premier Substitut du Procureur de la République près le Tribunal de Grande Instance, 46 rue de Fécamp, 75102 PARIS (France)

Mr Árpád GÖNCZ, President of the Republic of Hungary (Hungary)

Mr Kálmán GYÖRGYI, Prosecutor General of the Republic of Hungary, Office of the Prosecutor General of Hungary (Hungary)

Mr Attila HLAVATHY, Director, Prosecutor General's Office, Marko u. 16, H-1055 BUDAPEST, (Hungary),

Ms Nóra Katalin BONOMI, Prosecutor at the Office of the Prosecutor General (Hungary)

Mr László LÁNG, Director, Prosecutor General's Office (Hungary)

Ms Iiona LÉVAI, Prosecutor, Prosectuor General's Office (Hungary)

M. Christian PAUL-LOUBIÈRE, Magistrat au Tribunal de grande instance de Paris, Chargé de Travaux dirigés, Panthéon-Corbonne Paris I, 4 Boulevard du Palais, 75055 PARIS RP

M. José Manuel SANTOS PAIS, Bureau de Documentation et de Droit comparé, Bureau de Procureur Général , Rua vale de Pereiro 2-40, 1200, LISBONNE, (Portugal)

Mr Boyan Rangelov STANKOV, Professor of Criminology, Deputy President of the Council for Criminological Research, Genral Prosecutor's Office, Bul. Vitosha 2, 1000, SOFIA

Mr Jerzy SZYMANSKI, District Prosecutor's Office, ul Nanciycielska 10/33, 86-300 GRUDZIADZ

Ms Birgitte VESTBERG, Staatsadvokaten for Fyn, Sydostsjeelland, Lolland, Falster og Bornholm, Jens Kofodsgade 1, 3, tv, DK-1268 KOBENHAVN K (Denmark)

Mr Peter WILKITZKI, Ministerialrat, Bundesministerium de Justiz, Postfach 200 365, D-53170 BONN 2 (Germany)

## OBSERVERS

Mr Werner ROTH, Chief Prosecutor, Rechtendachweg 1, Schlangenpad, DÜSSELDORF, D-65388 (Germany)

## SECRETARIAT

Mme Marie-Odile WIEDERKEHR, Directeur adjoint des Affaires Juridiques

Mlle Nathalie WAWRZYNIAK, Conseiller de Programme, Direction des Affaires Juridiques

Ms Claire GROVE, Secretary, Directorate of Legal Affairs

# Sales agents for publications of the Council of Europe
## Agents de vente des publications du Conseil de l'Europe

**AUSTRALIA/AUSTRALIE**
Hunter publications, 58A, Gipps Street
AUS-3066 COLLINGWOOD, Victoria
Fax: (61) 34 19 71 54

**AUSTRIA/AUTRICHE**
Gerold und Co., Graben 31
A-1011 WIEN 1
Fax: (43) 1512 47 31 29

**BELGIUM/BELGIQUE**
La Librairie européenne SA
50, avenue A. Jonnart
B-1200 BRUXELLES 20
Fax: (32) 27 35 08 60

Jean de Lannoy
202, avenue du Roi
B-1060 BRUXELLES
Fax: (32) 25 38 08 41

**CANADA**
Renouf Publishing Company Limited
1294 Algoma Road
CDN-OTTAWA ONT K1B 3W8
Fax: (1) 613 741 54 39

**DENMARK/DANEMARK**
Munksgaard
PO Box 2148
DK-1016 KØBENHAVN K
Fax: (45) 33 12 93 87

**FINLAND/FINLANDE**
Akateeminen Kirjakauppa
Keskuskatu 1, PO Box 218
FIN-00381 HELSINKI
Fax: (358) 01 21 44 35

**GERMANY/ALLEMAGNE**
UNO Verlag
Poppelsdorfer Allee 55
D-53115 BONN
Fax: (49) 228 21 74 92

**GREECE/GRÈCE**
Librairie Kauffmann
Mavrokordatou 9, GR-ATHINAI 106 78
Fax: (30) 13 83 03 20

**HUNGARY/HONGRIE**
Euro Info Service
Magyarorszag
Margitsziget (Europa Haz),
H-1138 BUDAPEST
Fax: (36) 1 111 62 16

**IRELAND/IRLANDE**
Government Stationery Office
4-5 Harcourt Road, IRL-DUBLIN 2
Fax: (353) 14 75 27 60

**ISRAEL/ISRAËL**
ROY International
PO Box 13056
IL-61130 TEL AVIV
Fax: (972) 3 546 1442

**ITALY/ITALIE**
Libreria Commissionaria Sansoni
Via Duca di Calabria, 1/1
Casella Postale 552, I-50125 FIRENZE
Fax: (39) 55 64 12 57

**MALTA/MALTE**
L. Sapienza & Sons Ltd
26 Republic Street
PO Box 36
VALLETTA CMR 01
Fax: (356) 246 182

**NETHERLANDS/PAYS-BAS**
InOr-publikaties, PO Box 202
NL-7480 AE HAAKSBERGEN
Fax: (31) 542 72 92 96

**NORWAY/NORVÈGE**
Akademika, A/S Universitetsbokhandel
PO Box 84, Blindern
N-0314 OSLO
Fax: (47) 22 85 30 53

**PORTUGAL**
Livraria Portugal, Rua do Carmo, 70
P-1200 LISBOA
Fax: (351) 13 47 02 64

**SPAIN/ESPAGNE**
Mundi-Prensa Libros SA
Castelló 37, E-28001 MADRID
Fax: (34) 15 75 39 98

Llibreria de la Generalitat
Rambla dels Estudis, 118
E-08002 BARCELONA
Fax: (34) 34 12 18 54

**SWEDEN/SUÈDE**
Aktiebolaget CE Fritzes
Regeringsgatan 12, Box 163 56
S-10327 STOCKHOLM
Fax: (46) 821 43 83

**SWITZERLAND/SUISSE**
Buchhandlung Heinimann & Co.
Kirchgasse 17, CH-8001 ZÜRICH
Fax: (41) 12 51 14 81

BERSY
Route du Manège 60, CP 4040
CH-1950 SION 4
Fax: (41) 27 31 73 32

**TURKEY/TURQUIE**
Yab-Yay Yayimcilik Sanayi Dagitim Tic Ltd
Barbaros Bulvari 61 Kat 3 Daire 3
Beşiktaş, TR-ISTANBUL

**UNITED KINGDOM/ROYAUME-UNI**
HMSO, Agency Section
51 Nine Elms Lane
GB-LONDON SW8 5DR
Fax: (44) 171 873 82 00

**UNITED STATES and CANADA/
ÉTATS-UNIS et CANADA**
Manhattan Publishing Company
468 Albany Post Road
PO Box 850
CROTON-ON-HUDSON, NY 10520, USA
Fax: (1) 914 271 58 56

**STRASBOURG**
Librairie Kléber
Palais de l'Europe
F-67075 Strasbourg Cedex
Fax: (33) 88 52 91 21

---

Council of Europe Publishing/Éditions du Conseil de l'Europe
Council of Europe/Conseil de l'Europe
F-67075 Strasbourg Cedex
Tel. (33) 88 41 25 81 - Fax (33) 88 41 27 80